Updated 2022

# Egyptian Musical Instruments

Second Edition

Moustafa Gadalla

**Egyptian Musical Instruments**, 2nd Edition
by Moustafa Gadalla

This book is the second edition of the same title that was published in 2004.

All rights reserved. No part of this book may be reproduced or transmitted in any form or by any means, electronic or mechanical, including photocopying, recorded or by any information storage and retrieval system without written permission from the author, except for the inclusion of brief quotations in a review.

Copyright © 2004, 2017 , 2018, 2020 and 2022 by Moustafa Gadalla, All rights reserved.

# CONTENTS

About the Author .................................................................. v

Preface [2nd Edition] ........................................................... vii

Preface [1st Edition] ............................................................ ix

Standards and Terminology ................................................ x

Map of Egypt ..................................................................... xii

PART I. MAIN BODY

1. The Wealth of Instruments ............................................ 1
   1.1 The Egyptian Instruments ........................................ 1
   1.2 General Characteristics of Egyptian Instruments ..... 6
   1.3 Musicians in Ancient (and Present-Day) Egypt ....... 7
   1.4 The Musical Orchestra ............................................. 8

2. Stringed Instruments .................................................. 11
   2.1 General ............................................................... 11
   2.2 Lyres ................................................................... 12
   2.3 Tri-gonon/Tri-qanon (Zither) ......................... 15
   2.4 Harps .................................................................. 17
   2.5 Tanbouras (String Instruments with Neck) ........... 27

3. Wind Instruments ..................................................... 45
   3.1 The Magic Nay (End-Blown Flute) ....................... 46
   3.2 Transverse Flute ................................................ 51
   3.3 Pan Flute ............................................................ 52
   3.4 Single Reed Pipe (Clarinet) .............................. 53
   3.5 Double Pipes ..................................................... 54
   3.6 The Twin Horns/Trumpets ................................. 63

4. Percussion Instruments ........................................... 67
   4.1 Membrano-Phone Instruments ............................. 67
   4.2 Non-Membrano-Phone (Idiophone) ..................... 73
   Instruments
   4.3 Human Parts (hands, fingers, thighs, feet, etc.) ...... 81

5. The Musical Performance ........................................ 84
   5.1 The Harmonic Merit Hand ................................. 84
   5.2 The Written Sounds ........................................... 87
   5.3 The Rhythmic Timing ........................................ 90
   5.4 Moods and Modes .............................................. 95

Glossary ........................................................................ 99

Selected Bibliography .............................................. 103

Sources and Notes ..................................................... 107

1

## ABOUT THE AUTHOR

Moustafa Gadalla is an Egyptian-American independent Egyptologist who was born in Cairo, Egypt in 1944. He holds a Bachelor of Science degree in civil engineering from Cairo University.

From his early childhood, Gadalla pursued his Ancient Egyptian roots with passion, through continuous study and research. Since 1990, he has dedicated and concentrated all his time to researching and writing.

Gadalla is the author of twenty-two published internationally acclaimed books about the various aspects of the Ancient Egyptian history and civilization and its influences worldwide. In addition he operates a multimedia resource center for accurate, educative studies of Ancient Egypt, presented in an engaging, practical, and interesting manner that appeals to the general public.

He was the Founder of Tehuti Research Foundation which was later incorporated into the multi-lingual Egyptian Wisdom Center (https://www.egyptianwisdomcenter.org) in more than ten languages. He is also the Founder and Head of the online Egyptian Mystical University (https://www.EgyptianMysticalUniversity.org). Another ongoing activity has been his creation and production of performing arts projects such as the Isis Rises Operetta (https://www.isisrisesoperetta.com); to be followed soon by Horus The Initiate Operetta; as well other productions.

2

# PREFACE [2ND EDITION]

This book is a revised and enhanced edition of the originally published book *Egyptian Musical Instruments*, by Moustafa Gadalla, in 2004. This new edition expands and adds to previous texts of the first edition.

This book shows the wealth of the Ancient Egyptian musical instruments and their ranges and playing techniques; as well as short overviews about the musicians and how the musical orchestra followed hand signals and written musical notations.

This book consists of five chapters:

*Chapter 1*: **The Wealth of Instruments** will cover the general characteristics of Egyptian instruments as well the major components of the musical orchestra

*Chapter 2*: **Stringed Instruments** will cover various Ancient Egyptian stringed instruments such as lyres, trigonon (zither), Harps including playing techniques: Harps—Playing Techniques; The All-Encompassing

Capacities of Ancient; string instruments with neck—such as short-neck Lute; the long-neck Egyptian guitars; and Bowed Instruments [Kamanga, Rababa].

*Chapter 3*: **Wind Instruments** will cover The end blown flute; transverse flute; pan flute; single reed pipe (clarinet); double Pipe; double clarinet; double oboe; arghool; others (bagpipe and organ); and horns/trumpets.

*Chapter 4*: **Percussion Instruments** will cover the membrano-phone instruments such as drums and tambourines; and the non-membrano-phone (idiophone) instruments such as percussion sticks, clappers, sistrums/ sistra, cymbals, castanets, bells (chimes), xylophone and glockenspiel and human parts (hands, fingers, thighs, feet, etc.).

*Chapter 5*: **The Musical Performance** will cover the significance and roles of the fingers and their knuckles in producing and directing musical performances; as well as the varied methods for maintaining the rhythmic timing/ tempo—including the use of syllables.

It should be noted that the digital edition of this book as published in PDF and E-book formats have a substantial number of photographs that compliment the text materials throughout the book.

Moustafa Gadalla

3

# PREFACE [1ST EDITION]

Our book *Egyptian Rhythm: The Heavenly Melodies* presents the cosmic roots of Egyptian musical, vocal, and dancing rhythmic forms. It also details the fundamentals (theory and practice) of music in the typical Egyptian way: simple, coherent, and comprehensive. In addition, it provides a detailed description of the major Egyptian musical instruments and their playing techniques, functions, etc. It also elaborates on Egyptian rhythmic practices in all aspects of their lives.

We have noted that many readers may not be interested in the detailed theory and practices of music in Ancient Egypt. Therefore, we decided to publish a separate book showing the wealth of the Ancient Egyptian musical instruments and their ranges and playing techniques. We also included short overviews about the musicians and how the musical orchestra followed hand signals and written musical notations.

Moustafa Gadalla

4

# STANDARDS AND TERMINOLOGY

1. Throughout this book, octave ranges are named according to the following system:

c3 c2 c1 c c1 c2 c3

<— Lower Octaves -<—|—>- Higher Octaves—>

2. Capital letters (C, D, E, etc.) are reserved for general pitch names without regard to a specific octave range.

3. The Ancient Egyptian word neter and its feminine form netert have been wrongly, and possibly intentionally, translated to god and goddess by almost all academicians. Neteru (plural of neter/netert) are the divine principles and functions of the One Supreme God.

4. You may find variations in writing the same Ancient Egyptian term, such as Amen/Amon/Amun or Pir/Per. This is because the vowels you see in translated Egyptian texts are only approximations of sounds which are used by Western Egyptologists to help them pronounce the Ancient Egyptian terms/words.

5. We will be using the most commonly recognized words for the English-speaking people that identify a neter/netert [god, goddess] or a pharaoh or a city; followed by other 'variations' of such a word/term.

It should be noted that the real names of the deities (gods, goddesses) were kept secret so as to guard the cosmic power of the deity. The Neteru were referred to by epithets that describe particular qualities, attributes and/or aspect(s) of their roles. Such applies to all common terms such as Isis, Osiris, Amun, Re, Horus, etc.

6. When using the Latin calendar, we will use the following terms:

> **BCE** – Before Common Era. Also noted in other references as BC.
> **CE** – Common Era. Also noted in other references as AD.

7. The term Baladi will be used throughout this book to denote the present silent majority of Egyptians that adhere to the Ancient Egyptian traditions. [See *Ancient Egyptian Culture Revealed* by Moustafa Gadalla for detailed information.]

5

**MAP OF EGYPT**

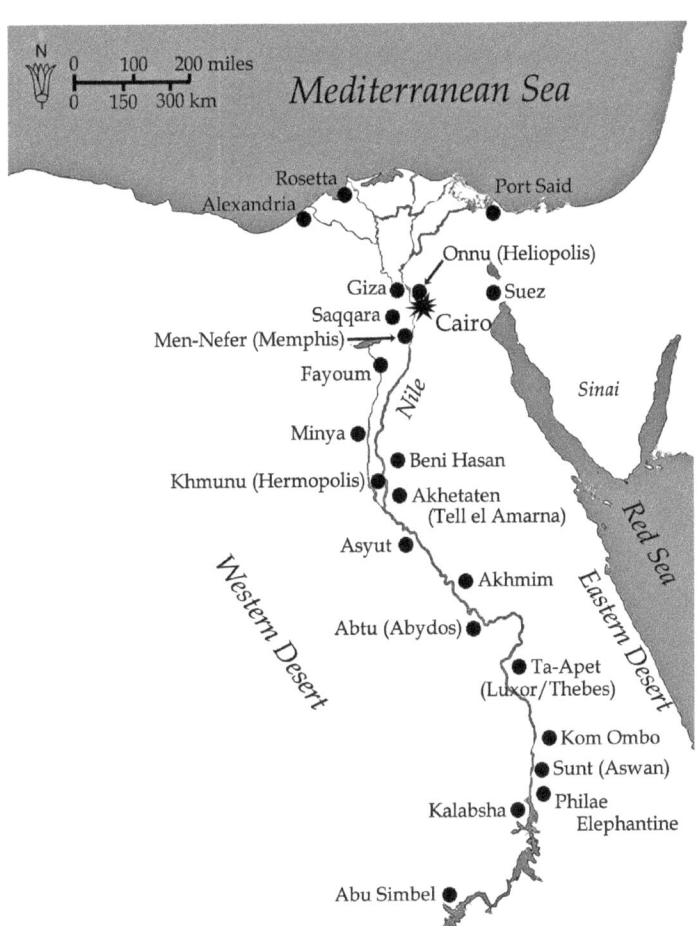

# 1

# The Wealth of Instruments

## 1.1 THE EGYPTIAN INSTRUMENTS

The archaeological and traditional Egyptian history of music is much more abundant than in any other country. The wall reliefs of the Ancient Egyptian temples and tombs depict numerous types and forms of musical instruments, the technique in which these instruments were to be played and tuned, ensemble playing, and much, much more. These musical scenes visibly show the hands of the harp player striking certain strings

and the wind instrument players playing certain chords together.

The distances between the lute frets clearly show that the corresponding intervals and scales can be measured and calculated.

The positions of the harpists' hands on the strings plainly indicate ratios such as the Fourth, the Fifth, and the Octave, revealing an unquestionable knowledge of the laws governing musical harmony.

The playing of musical instruments is also depicted as being controlled by conductors' hand movements, which also help us identify certain tones and intervals and functions of sound.

The intervals of Fourth, Fifth, and Octave were the most common in Ancient Egyptian representations. Curt Sachs [in his book, *History of Musical Instruments*] found that out of 17 harpists represented on Egyptian art works (with sufficient realism and distinctness to be reliable records), seven are striking a Fourth chord, five a Fifth chord, and five an Octave chord.

The most frequently depicted harps were found to have seven strings and, according to Curt Sachs' study of Egyptian instruments, the Egyptians tuned their harps in the same diatonic series of intervals.

One of the two harps depicted in Ramses III's tomb [shown below] has 13 strings; where if the longest string represented pros-lambanomenos (or D), the remaining 12 strings would more than **supply all the tones, semi-tones, and quarter-tones, of the diatonic, chromatic, and enharmonic genera; within the compass of an octave.**

In addition to the numerous representations of musical scenes pictured in temples and tombs from all periods throughout Egypt's dynastic history, we also have access to hundreds of various Ancient Egyptian musical instruments which have been recovered from their tombs. These Egyptian instruments are now spread in museums and private collections throughout the world.

Most of these instruments were found to be carefully and individually wrapped in cloth before they were placed in the tombs.

All these findings, together with early historian writings of Egyptian musical heritage as well as the traditions of modern Nile inhabitants, corroborate to provide a most authentic account of the musical history of Ancient Egypt.

Unfortunately, much of this CLEARLY EGYPTIAN evidence has been distorted time and time again throughout history, by Western academia. On the subject of Ancient Egypt, practically all Western academicians have contempt and envy towards this great civilization. The typical Western academician will simultaneously: 1) describe Egyptians as being very conservative, who didn't change or evolve and who had no imagination, etc.; and 2) describe the achievements in Ancient Egypt as being borrowed/stolen/copied from non-Egyptians. It is irrational for anyone to simultaneously employ these contradictory arguments.

The fact is that Egyptians (Ancient and Baladi) are remarkably traditionalist to a fault, as attested to by ALL early historians, such as Herodotus, who, in *The Histories*, Book Two, 79, states:

> *"The Egyptians keep to their native customs and never adopt any from abroad."*

Herodotus, in *The Histories*, Book Two, 91, also states:

> *"The Egyptians are unwilling to adopt Greek customs, or, to speak generally, those of any other country."*

## 1.2 GENERAL CHARACTERISTICS OF EGYPTIAN INSTRUMENTS

1. The musical scenes depicted in Ancient Egyptian tombs, as well as instruments found from the Old and Middle Kingdoms, indicate ratios between the open strings of the harp and the densely-ordered frets on the long necks of string instruments, as well as measurements between the finger-holes in wind instruments. These reveal/confirm that:

> a. Several types of musical scales were known/used.

> b. Narrow-stepped scales were common from the earliest known Egyptian history (more than 5,000 years ago).

> c. The playing and tuning techniques of string instruments provided for the solo and chordal playing of instruments.

> d. The playing techniques of wind instruments produced small increments and the organ effect.

> e. Both the cyclic (up-and-down) method and the divisive method of tuning were in use.

2. The Ancient Egyptians were/are famed worldwide for mastering the playing techniques of their musical instruments. Egyptians skills in the use of these instruments was affirmed by Athenaeus, who stated (in his texts [iv,

25]) that *"both the Greeks and "barbarians" were taught music by Egyptian natives."*

After the demise of the Ancient Egyptian Pharaonic Era, Egypt continued to be the learning center for music, for the Arabized/Islamized countries.

## 1.3 MUSICIANS IN ANCIENT (AND PRESENT-DAY) EGYPT

Musicians in Ancient and Baladi Egypt were/are highly regarded. The Ancient Egyptian neteru (gods) themselves are depicted on the temple walls, playing musical instruments. The profession of a musician was an obvious sign and practical consequence of the significant functions of music in Egyptian society.

Musicians had various and distinctive roles. Some of their many musical titles included: overseer, instructor, director of musicians, teacher, musicians of Ma-at, *mistress of the neteru*, musicians of Amun, musicians of the Great Ennead, musicians of Hathor, etc. The profession of the chironomid (conductor/maestro) was also noted in Ancient Egyptian literature.

The musical profession has comprised the whole range of representatives of the temples and other societal activities. There were various and well-trained groups of singers and dancers who learned and practiced the set performance rules suitable for various occasions.

Diodorus of Sicily wrote about Horus Behdety [Apollo] and his nine muses in *Book I* [18, 4-5]:

*"Osiris was laughter-loving and fond of music and the*

*dance; consequently he took with him a multitude of musicians, among whom were nine maidens who could sing and were trained in the other arts, these maidens being those who are called the Muses; and their leader (hegetes), as the account goes, was Horus Behdety (Apollo), who was for that reason also given the name Musegetes."*

Diodorus' account provides us with two interesting points:

1. The title of Horus Behdety is noted as *Muse-getes*, which is an Egyptian term meaning musician. *Musegete/Muse-kate* is not an Arabic word.

2. The concept of nine muses is of Egyptian origin, as it relates to Ancient Egyptian deities.

A great number of musicians in present-day Egypt belong to the mystical Sufi groups. They perform in weddings, circumcisions, countless annual festivals (mouleds), funerals, etc. They are all well-disciplined musicians, dancers, reciters, and singers, just like their ancestors. If they are not blind, they perform with blindfolded or closed eyes.

In the Ancient Egyptian musical scenes, most musicians are shown blind, vision impaired, or blindfolded—to exalt the metaphysical aspect of music.

## 1.4 THE MUSICAL ORCHESTRA

Musical instruments differ in compass, variety of strength of a single note, accent value, survival value, speed of articulation for a repeated note, and how many notes each instrument can play at once. As such, a variety of instruments were utilized by the Ancient Egyptians, to provide a complete system/range of musical sounds.

It should be noted that the overview of Ancient Egyptian musical instruments in this book is limited to instruments that can be compared with present-day instruments.

Some of the instruments of the Ancient Egyptians differ too much from the present day classification to be classed with any of them.

Musical bands varied in Ancient Egypt. Smaller and larger ensembles were employed for various purposes, as evident from musical scenes depicted in Ancient Egyptian buildings. It is sufficiently evident, from the sculptures of the Ancient Egyptians, that their musicians were acquainted with the triple symphony—the harmony of instruments, voices, and of voices and instruments. The playing of musical instruments was controlled by the conductors' hand movements (chironomids). Their hand signs show a variety of playing: unison, chord, polyphony, etc., as stated in chapter 5.

The Egyptian orchestra/ensemble generally consisted of four instrument groups:

> 1. String instruments with open strings, like trigonon, lyre, harp, etc. [See Chapter 2.]
>
> 2. String instruments with stopped strings on a neck, like the tanboura, guitar, oud/lute, etc. [See Chapter 2.]

3. Wind instruments like the flute, pipe, etc. [See Chapter 3.]

4. Percussion instruments like drums, clappers, bells, etc. [See Chapter 4.]

The following chapters detail found and depicted Ancient Egyptian instruments, as categorized above.

# 2

# Stringed Instruments

## 2.1 GENERAL

Ancient Egyptian stringed instruments consist of basically two groups:

1. Those with open strings: lyres, harps, zithers, etc. This group is usually tuned by ear in a cycle of fifths and fourths. Tuning is done by selecting a string (C) and tuning another string to its upper Perfect Fifth (G), then reverting to (D) a Fourth down, and going up to (A) by another Fifth, and so on. This difference between a Fifth and a Fourth is called a major whole tone, which is equal to 203.77 cents.

2. Those with stopped strings: instruments with well-defined necks such as tanbouras, guitars, etc. This group is governed by the divisive method of tuning. Tuning is accomplished by stopping strings along the neck at proportioned distances (by use of frets), as follows:

> 1/2 the length to get the Octave
> 1/3 the length to get the Fifth
> 1/4 the length to get the Fourth

There are, however, lyres, harps, and zithers with strings

occasionally stopped, and tanbouras with open strings, as explained in the Ka-nun playing technique [later on this chapter], and as will be explained in the harp playing techniques later on this chapter.

## 2.2 LYRES

Ancient Egyptian lyres have a yoke-shaped frame consisting of two arms and a crossbar that project from the upper side of the body.

There were two main types of lyres in Ancient Egypt:

1. Asymmetrical shape, which has two divergent asymmetrical arms, an oblique crossbar, and a soundbox.

2. Symmetrical rectangular shape, which has two parallel arms, a crossbar at right angles, and the soundbox.

The quality of the sound of both types was influenced by the soundbox, which was basically square or trapezoid in outline.

Many Egyptian lyres were of considerable power, having 5, 7, 10, and 18 strings.

They were usually supported between the elbow and the side, and were played with the hand and/or the plectrum. The plectrum was made of tortoiseshell, bone, ivory, or wood, and was often attached to the lyre by a string.

The numerous depictions of lyre playing techniques correspond with the technique of present-day playing. The lyre was held at a slant or even horizontally, away from the player.

The pressure of the fingers stretched the strings and thus altered the pitch. The right hand scratched with a plectrum over all strings at once, while the fingers of the left hand, stretched against the strings, deadened those that were not wanted.

The Egyptian lyres had a compass of several octaves which contain the unique Egyptian musical increments.

Smaller tones were produced similar to the harp playing techniques described later on in this chapter.

There are perfectly preserved wooden lyres [now in the Berlin and Leiden museums]. In the Leiden collection, the two limbs of the lyres are adorned by horses' heads. Their design, form, principle, and alternate long and short strings resemble some of those depicted in several Ancient Egyptian tombs.

The following are additional examples of depicted/found Ancient Egyptian lyres:

> • Bes, recognized since the pre-dynastic era [prior to 3000 BCE], is shown in a bronze statuette striking the strings of an asymmetrical lyre with a plectrum [now in the Cairo Museum, cat. #41736].

- A symmetrical lyre was identified by Hans Hickmann in a 6$^{th}$ Dynasty tomb [2323-2150 BCE, Saqqara].

- Asymmetrical lyres from the Middle Kingdom [2040-1783 BCE] are depicted in the tombs of Beni Hassan.

- An asymmetrical lyre was found bearing an inscription to Amenhotep I [16$^{th}$ century BCE].

- A symmetrical 14-stringed lyre is depicted in the tomb of Kynebu [dated to the 12$^{th}$ century BCE], reminiscent of surviving Ancient Egyptian lyres [now in the Berlin and Leiden Museums].

## 2.3 TRI-GONON/TRI-QANON (ZITHER)

Flavius Josephus, in his volumes *History of the Jews*, stated that the Ancient Egyptian temple musicians played an enharmonic triangular instrument (órganon trígonon enarmónion). The trígonon consists of two terms, tri and gonon. The term 'tri' is indicative of the form and nature of this unique Egyptian instrument, which is:

- Shaped in a triangular form, which some call trapezoidal, because the shortest string must have a length in order to produce a sound.

- The arrangement of the strings in triplets. Each of the three strings has different thicknesses, and all three are tuned in unison.

The qanon has played an extremely important role in Egypt, as testified by Flavius Josephus.

- There is an Ancient Egyptian raft zither at the Museum for Ethnology and Prehistory [Hamburg, Germany].

- Qanon was mentioned by al-Farabi [10$^{th}$ century CE] to be an instrument of 45 strings (15 triplets) that was already in existence in his time.

- Qanon was never referred to as an instrument of any other origin but Egypt; and Egypt is still recognized as the best builder of this instrument. The instrument's name, qanon, appears in one of the oldest stories of *The Arabian Nights*, the tale of Ali ibn Bakkar and Shams al-Nahar (169th night), which is ascribed to the 10th century. An epithet to its name, **Missri**, indicates **Massr** (or Egypt) as its home.

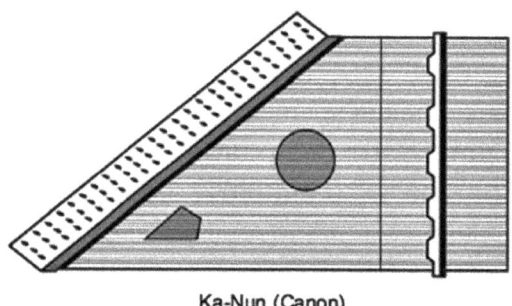

Ka-Nun (Canon)

The present form of the qanon is a flat box with a triangular-shaped body of strings. It varies from 21 to 28 triple strings (a total of 63 to 84 strings), but the most common consists of 26 triplets (78 strings). Each triplet is tuned in unison.

The strings are plucked with tortoise-shell plectra which are affixed to rings that are worn on the right and left index fingers. The right hand plays the melody and the left hand doubles it in the lower octave, except for those passages where it stops a string to raise its pitch. The instrument has detachable metal bridges that can be placed beneath the strings to alter their length and therefore their tuning. Playing techniques can also follow the same techniques for lyres and harps [more details later this chapter].

The Egyptian orchestra tunes both types (cyclic and divisive) of string instruments by using the Egyptian qanon (zither), which is the instrument that other instruments in the orchestra tune to because it follows both principles at once: it has open strings that follow the cyclic system of tuning, while the melody string follows the divisive system. The melody string is fretted not by actual raised frets, but by marking stopping places along the soundboard.

## 2.4 HARPS

The Ancient Egyptian harps varied greatly in form, size, and the number of their strings. They are represented in the ancient paintings with 4, 6, 7, 8, 9, 10, 11, 12, 14, 17, 20, 21, and 22 strings.

The harp was thought to be especially suited for temple service. It was even shown in the hands of the deities themselves.

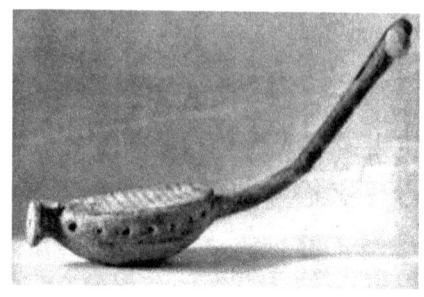

There were basically two types of harps:

1. The small portable (shoulder) harp (shallow arch). Shoulder harps are found in large numbers in muse-

ums throughout the world. Like all instruments of the sort, they had a setting that could be moved from front to back; from top to bottom or vice-versa. It was a kind of suspension rod for the strings which allowed for a quick tuning to different pitches.

2. The larger, arched (bow) harp or angular harp. There have been several variations of the large harps in Egypt, such as in their structures and sizes, depending on the string holder and whether it lies on the top or bottom and whether the resonator is straight-lined or bent. [Shown herein is a scene from the tomb of Amenemhet, Beni Hasan, 12th Dynasty—c. 1850 BCE.]

There is barely any difference between the bow (arch) and angular harp, as far as their sound is concerned.

A few examples of found and depicted Ancient Egyptian harps are listed below:

- The tomb of Debhen from Giza [c. 2550 BCE] depicts two bow harps with well defined sound bodies.

- A huge bow harp is depicted in a relief from the tomb of Seshemnofer [Giza, 5$^{th}$ Dynasty, c. 2500 BCE].

- A bow harp is depicted in a scene from the tomb of Ti [c. 2400 BCE] at Saqqara.

- A bow harp is depicted in the Ptah-hotep tomb [c. 2400 BCE]. The scene shows 2-tone playing [also see chapter 5].

- A harp is depicted in a relief from the tomb of Nekauhor [2390 BCE, Saqqara, now at the Metropolitan Museum of Art, New York]. The scene shows 3-tone playing of music [also see chapter 5].

• 5 harp players in polyphonic playing are depicted in Idut's tomb, [c. 2320 BCE] at Saqqara.

• The consort of the deceased Mereruka [c. 2290 BCE] is shown playing a large harp in Mereruka's tomb in Saqqara. She is playing two different strings of the harp—polyphony [also see chapter 5].

• A bow harp is depicted in Rekhmire's tomb [c. 1420 BCE], in Luxor (Thebes). The string pegs are neatly depicted in the form of a modern trumpet mouthpiece.

• A bow harp is depicted in the tomb of Nakht [15$^{th}$ century BCE], Luxor (Thebes).

• Two musicians are shown playing two huge forms of the bowed harp in the tomb of Ramses III [1194-1163 BCE], Luxor (Thebes). Because of the two harp players, this tomb was called *The Harpers Tomb*, and the harps are known as *Bruce's Harps*. One harp is shown herein. [The other harp is shown on later on this chapter.]

- Ramses III is depicted offering a harp, in the sanctuary of the temple of Medinet Habu, in western Luxor (Thebes).

## Harp Playing Techniques

The strings of harps were always plucked with the fingers or a plectrum.

Ancient Egyptians were familiar with a whole series of playing techniques, as evident from tombs throughout Ancient Egypt's dynastic history. Both one-handed and two-handed playing techniques are presented, as follows:

### 1. One-Handed Playing

With harps, every note has an individual 'open' string. The one-handed technique is based on the divisive method of obtaining musical notes by stopping the string at certain proportional lengths. When this method is applied to the harp, only one hand is manipulating (shortening) the string for a specific ratio, which allows the other hand to pluck the shortened string (providing the note).

In order to locate the exact proportioned length of the string, and to ensure a firm contact at the proportional point, one of the left-hand fingers stretches and presses the string for the proportioned distance against a rod-shaped object (like a fingerboard), thereby shortening (stopping) the vibrating length of the string. The left hand was guided by frets, which were loops tied about the fingerboard at given points. The shortened length of this particular string can then be struck to produce the sound.

This one-handed technique allows an unlimited possibility of tones.

There are many examples of harpers performing this technique. They clearly show that the plucked string forms a slight angle. Examples:

- In a relief [shown below] from tomb 11 in the Luxor (Thebes) area [New Kingdom 1520 BCE], a Harper shortens the string with one hand and plucks with the other. The bent string is clearly shown.

- In Idut's Tomb [c. 2320 BCE], two of the five depicted harpists pluck with only the right hand, while the left one holds down the string.

## 2. Two-Handed Playing

The two-handed technique is based on the ability to pluck each open string with one of the player's fingers. Both hands can pluck the strings either individually, simultaneously, or one after the other; i.e. playing a chord or polyphony. Unwanted strings can be further dampened (muted) with the palm of the other hand.

## The All-Encompassing Capacities of Ancient Egyptian Harps

The numerous varieties of Ancient Egyptian harps reveals the wealth of their music-producing capabilities. The following overview is based on the ratio between open strings only.

**=> It should be noted that many more, smaller musical tones can be achieved by the one-handed playing technique, as shown earlier.**

1. With harps of 4 to 22 strings, some harps would have been capable of producing a wide range of notes for several octaves. The ratio between the shortest and longest is 1:3 to 1:4 (i.e. 1 to 2 octaves). With the one-handed playing technique, unlimited possibilities of various tones and octaves can be achieved.

2. The intervals of Fourth, Fifth, and Octave were

the most common in Ancient Egyptian representations. Curt Sachs [in his book, *History of Musical Instruments*] found that out of 17 harpists represented on Egyptian art works with sufficient realism and distinctness to be reliable records, seven are striking a Fourth chord, five a Fifth chord, and five an Octave chord.

3. The ratio between the shortest and the longest string of several Ancient Egyptian harps is about 2:3. As this interval is divided between five strings, the scale would provide a range of tones between half and full tones. On harps with ten strings, this would give an average interval of a (minor) semitone (90 cents = 4 commas).

4. One of the two harps found in Ramses III's tomb has 13 strings, whereby if the longest string represented proslambanomenos, or D; the remaining 12 strings would more than supply all the tones, semitones, and quarter-tones, of the diatonic, chromatic, and enharmonic genera, within the compass of an octave.

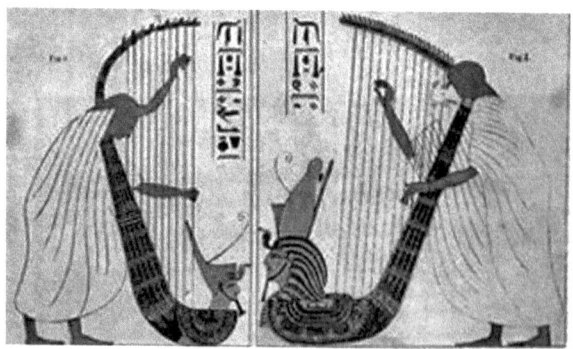

The tuning of this 13-string harp can furnish the

four tetrachords, hypaton, meson, synemmenon, and diezeugnenon, with proslambanomenos at the bottom:

5. The most frequently depicted harps were found to have seven strings, and according to Curt Sachs' study of the Egyptian instruments, the Egyptians tuned their harps in the same diatonic series of intervals.

6. An Ancient Egyptian harp with 20 strings [found in Luxor (Thebes)] shows the pentatonic scale running through four octaves. And the harp with 21 strings [in the Paris Museum] had the same order of intervals, with the addition of the keynote at the top.

## 2.5 TANBOURAS (STRING INSTRUMENTS WITH NECK)

The tanboura/tamboura is basically a string instrument with a well-defined long neck, which is used to stop the string at any desired length before striking it.

The tanboura is known by many other "names", such as tamboura or nabla. We will use tanboura here as a family name for string instruments with a defined neck. Such a family of instruments includes (but is not limited to) short neck lutes, long neck guitars, etc.

This tanboura-type instrument appears on numerous wall paintings, sculptured panels, scarabs, sarcophagi, and as an ornament on vases and boxes; and represents, in hieroglyphics, the single attribute *good/beautiful*.

A figure of the tanboura-type instrument is found among the Egyptian hieroglyphs, dating it to more than 5,000 years ago. The figure depicts two, and sometimes four, tuning pegs.

In Ancient Egypt, tanbouras led the religious processions, validating its present nickname as 'King of Instruments'. The tanboura with the short neck (known now by its "Arabic name", oud) continues to serve musical instructional purposes, acoustic demonstrations, musical theory, and is the cornerstone of concert, family, and folk music, including theater, movie and radio presentations.

There were numerous shapes and forms of stringed

instruments with defined necks. The neck length varied from the short type to the very long. The body shape varied from oval to pear to almond and many other shapes.

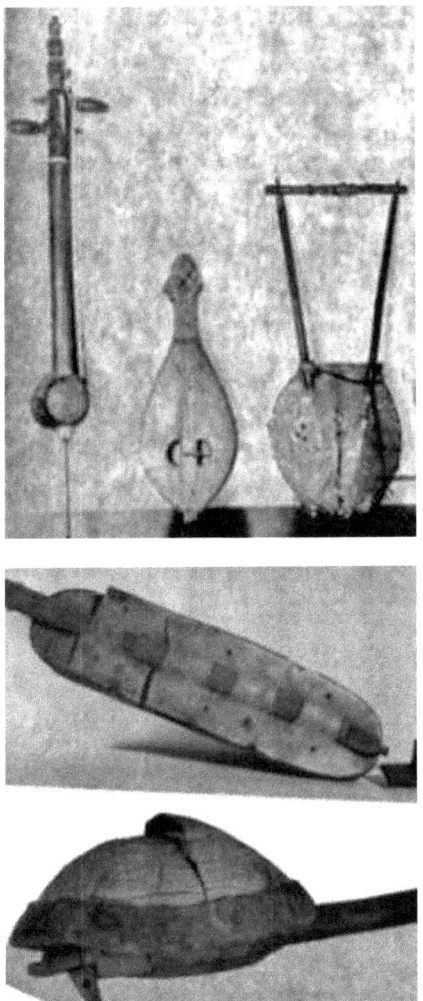

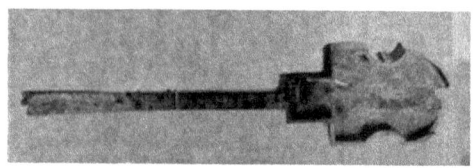

The Ancient Egyptians utilized tanboura-type string instruments in an unlimited manner, providing variation in sound and design, such as:

**A. Body Shapes**: The body shapes varied from an oval to one with sides slightly curved like present-day guitars or violins. They were also shaped like a tortoise shell or pear, with a flat or slightly rounded back. They all had sounding holes through the top or body of the instrument.

**B. Strings and Tuning**: Tuning pegs are clearly shown on the hieroglyphic symbols. Found instruments indicate the use of 2-5 pegs, which usually have tassels dangling from them. The tuning pegs of some tanbouras are shaped like the letter T, and are inserted from the front or the side. Many instruments were buried in the tombs without pegs or strings.

Ancient Egyptian tanbouras had strings of two, three, four, five, or six, which were made of catgut, silk, or horsetail threads. Strings were produced in different thicknesses. When all the strings of an instrument were of the same thickness, a tuning peg was needed for each string. When the thicknesses of the strings were varied proportionally, so as to provide the different musical ratios between the strings, fewer tuning pegs were required. As such, a tuning peg may control several strings (of variable thicknesses) that can be tuned in unison.

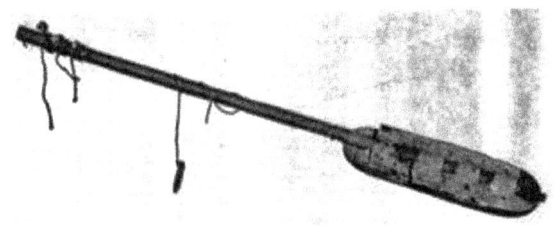

The tanboura-type instrument was played with a plectrum or bow.

**C. Length of Neck:** Some instruments have long necks (like a guitar) or short necks (like a lute or oud). The length of the short neck was as short as the body of the resonator. The length of the long neck was as long as 47 inches (120 cm), as in Harmosis' instrument.

**D. Fretting:** A musician shortened the vibrating lengths of the strings by pressing them against the neck to produce notes of different pitch. To assist in stopping the required proportioned length of the string, to provide a specific pitch, most instruments came with frets in a variety of forms in order to allow for flexibility of performance.

Since frets restrict the player to specific positions, stringed instruments played by well-trained musicians were often left without frets, so that the finger could glide freely along the fingerboard.

The frets of Ancient Egyptian instruments were either:

1. Easily shifted, by moving the fretting bands.

2. Lightly marked. The strings were thin enough and sufficiently high above the fingerboard to be conveniently driven up in pitch by adding pressure.

3. Only marked at some big intervals by bands, to outline the overall parameter and allow both guidance and flexibility. In addition, there were mobile frets that, together with these frets, divided the octave into smaller increments (such as 10, 17, 22) or more sections. An example is shown herein of Nakhtamun in Luxor (Thebes) [14th century BCE, Tomb 341].

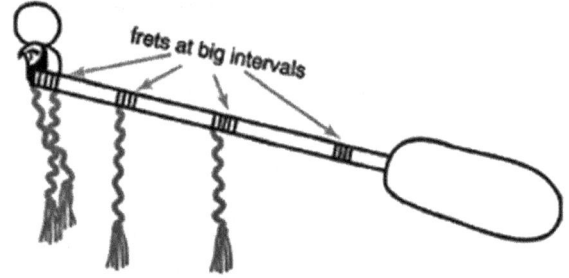

[See more examples later on in this chapter .]

4. Sometimes limited to the upper half of the neck, or sometimes extended down the neck to the body of the instrument. [Some examples are shown later on in this chapter.]

The flexibility of fretting techniques allows for:

1. The selection of any of the three types of tetrachords and frameworks [read *The Enduring Ancient Egyptian Musical System* by Moustafa Gadalla].

2. Increasing the instrument's capacity to produce numerous notes and consequently reducing the necessity to use more and different string instru-

ments in the musical ensemble to provide the different tetra-rchords and modes.

### Two-String Tanboura

Two strings were capable of producing a great number of notes. For instance, if these two strings were tuned Fourths to each other, they would furnish that series of sounds called hepta-chord, consisting of two conjunct tetra-chords, as B, c, d, e; E, f, g, a; and if the strings of this instrument were tuned Fifths, they would produce an octave, consisting of two disjunct tetra-chords.

This very Ancient Egyptian instrument (resembling its hieroglyphic symbol) proves that the Ancient Egyptians had discovered the means of extending their scale and multiplying the sounds of a few strings by the most simple and practical means.

Examples from the numerous Ancient Egyptian representations include:

> 1. A two-stringed tanboura with frets is depicted in a music scene in Luxor (Thebes) [Tomb 80, ca. 1450 BCE].

> 2. A two-stringed instrument appears in a music scene of a tomb in Luxor (Thebes) [Tomb 341, 14th century BCE].

### Three-String Tanboura

Three strings were common for the Ancient Egyptian tanboura-type instruments.

They were tuned in the Fourth, Fifth, and Octave. When each string is tuned in Fourths, the tanboura can reach a 2-octave range.

An example of this instrument was found in the tomb of Harmosis.

One of the most popular types in Ancient Egypt was the te-bouni, a banjo-like, three-stringed instrument with a moon-shaped body and parchment head.

### Four-String Tanboura

The Ancient Egyptian obelisk [now in Rome], which was built c. 1500 BCE, depicts a tanboura with four tuning pegs [shown herein].

Four-stringed tanboura-type instruments may have all their strings of the same thickness, in which case they were/are tuned in Fourths, to provide a compass of one or two Octaves.

The four strings with different thickness ratios of 6, 8, 9, 12 (tuned in unison) can provide all the necessary four pitches of the Octave, Fourth, Fifth, and sesquioctave (9:8).

The 4-stringed instrument continues to be popular in present-day Egypt.

**<u>Short-Neck Lute (present-day oud)</u>**

Ancient Egyptians were familiar with a type of shortneck lute with a sturdy pear-shaped body and a broad fingerboard. The number of strings ranged from two to six strings. Two lutes of this type came from Ancient Egyptian tombs in Luxor (Thebes) [dated c. 16th century BCE, now in the Berlin Museum], and are 14" (35 cm) and 19" (48.5 cm) long. The small one [shown herein] had 2, or possibly 3, strings. The larger one had 4 strings.

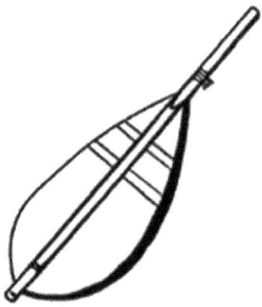

The most popular of this short-neck lute-type had/have four strings. Along with the frets, the instrument was/is able to provide the most popular 17-interval framework. This instrument is known today in the Arabized/Islamized countries as an oud.

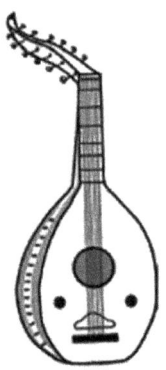

In addition to the above Egyptian instruments [now at the Berlin Museum], some other examples of this Ancient Egyptian instrument include:

> • A short neck type of lute is shown in a statuette of a lute player [New Kingdom, c. 3,500 years ago, now at the Cairo Museum, cat. #773].

- A statuette made of burnt clay shows a musician playing a short-neck lute [19-20th Dynasty, Cairo Museum, Cat. #38797].

**The Egyptian Guitars**

The Egyptian guitar consisted of two parts: a long flat neck, or handle, and a hollow oval body. Guitars are found depicted in numerous Ancient Egyptian tombs from all eras.

Four Ancient Egyptian strongly-notched, guitar-like instruments were found in the Qarara region, which dated to the Middle Kingdom [c. 2000 BCE]. In addition to one at Heidelberg, a complete instrument of that kind is found in the Cairo Museum, another in the Metropolitan Museum of Art in New York, and a smaller one in the collection of Moeck, Celle. They are designed for three to six strings.

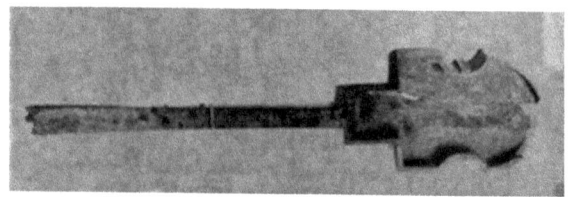

All these instruments are made of one piece. Only the necks of the larger examples are elongated with extension pieces, and all the instruments were provided with numerous frets.

It is from an ancient instrument of this kind, sometimes called cithara/kithara, that the modern name guitar (chitarra) has been derived. Their strongly lifted and tied-up, sound-producing body was the archetype for the present-day guitar.

### A Few Examples of Tanboura Variety

1. A tanboura-type instrument with seven frets is depicted in an Ancient Egyptian tomb from the Old Kingdom [ca. 4,500 years ago, now in the Berlin Museum]. The performer was therefore able to produce eight different intervals on each string. The spaces between the frets are painted in various colors.

2. Long-necked guitars, characterized by a long, extending and slightly laced resonance body are depicted in a music scene from the tomb of Pahekmen. Luxor (Thebes) [Tomb #343], 18th Dynasty [c. 16th century BCE].

3. A tanboura-type instrument with a 25" (62 cm) neck was found in Tomb 1389, Luxor (Thebes). [18th

Dynasty, ca. 16th century BCE, now in Cairo Museum, Cat. #69420.] The body is made of tortoise shell.

4. A large form of a long neck tanboura-type instrument, with a 47" (120 cm) long neck, was found in the tomb of Harmosis, [Thebes at Dêr el-Bahari, 16th century BCE, now at the Cairo Museum, Cat. #69421]. The instrument was made of a wooden, half-almond-formed resonator. Its three strings were tied at the bottom end to a specifically made projection. Then, the strings ran along a higher mechanism that could be moved back and forth.

5. Two tanboura-type instrument players are shown on a section from a wall painting in the tomb of Rekhmire [c. 1420 BCE, Luxor (Thebes)].

6. Long-necked instruments are played by a group in a part of a procession, depicted at the Temple of Luxor, from the time of Tut-Ankh-Amen [c. 1350 BCE].

7. A music scene from the tomb of Nebamun [Luxor (Thebes), 15th century BCE, now in the British Museum] depicts two types: a long-necked guitar with long almond-shaped resonator, and one with a rounded resonator. The latter appears to be made of a tortoise shell.

Both instruments here are provided with fingerboards. One has 8 visible frets, which begin halfway down the neck. The other has 17 visible frets [shown below].

8. A long-neck tanboura-type instrument is depicted in Luxor (Thebes) [Tomb 52, 15th century BCE], named after Nakht. The instrument has nine frets on its long neck, marked with bands. This instrument provides the span of a 10-interval framework.

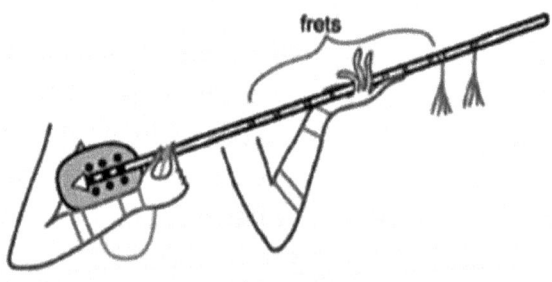

The measurement of the visible (not blocked by the player's hand) distances between some depicted frets yield the following intervals (in cents): 134–114–341–202–272; i.e. 6–5–15–9–12 Egyptian commas. The measured intervals are again consistent with the Egyptian musical comma as the measuring unit. It also shows the twin-octave system, a comma apart.

**Bowed Instruments (Kamanga, Rababa)**

There are several types and forms of bowed instruments, but they all follow the principle of the freely-swinging resonance strings that can be bowed or plucked. Bowed instruments had/have 1, 2, 3, or 4 strings. Two and four strings are the most common.

The strings of the instruments, as well as the bows, are made of horsetail hair. Horses have played a major role in the musical life of Ancient and Baladi Egypt. Several Ancient Egyptian instruments are adorned with figures of horses. The hair from horsetails—abundant and available to all—was/is used to produce music.

The typical way of playing all types and sizes of bowed instruments by the Ancient and Baladi Egyptians is to rest the body of the instrument on the thigh or on the floor and not under the chin, no matter how small the instrument is. The Egyptian way allows more control and the ability to turn (pivot) the instrument to produce the exact desired pitch and its duration.

Ancient Egyptian tombs show this Egyptian style of playing bowed instruments. In the tomb of Rekhmire [15th century BCE, Luxor (Thebes), Tomb #100], a female musician is depicted bowing the stringed instrument.

A similar scene is found in another tomb, where the instrument is resting on the player's thigh.

Bowed instruments are called kamanga. They had/have squared or rectangular bodies, and somewhat rounded backs. The form and structure of the kamanga is the same as the later, present-day violin.

Bowed instruments with two strings are called junior kamanga or ra-ba-ba—an Egyptian term meaning the Twin Soul (ba-ba) of the Creator (Ra). The Twin Soul (baba) is represented with two strings.

The rababa is a fiddle with a long fretless neck, and may be plucked or bowed. It has a short, narrow and cup-shaped body.

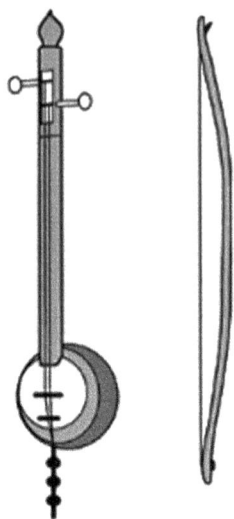

Rababas are very cheap to make as both the strings and the bow are made of horsetail hair. The resonating body can either be a carved coconut shell or wooden.

The bows of both the rababa and kamanga are made of a flexible elastic, slightly bent rod and horsehair.

Bowed instruments (such as kamanga and rababa) accompanied/accompany storytellers in Egypt because their sounds are the closest of all instruments to the nature of the human voice.

>>> Several photographs in support of the text of this chapter are to be found in the digital edition of this book as published in PDF and E-book formats.

3

# Wind Instruments

The Ancient Egyptian wind instruments can generally be classified into:

> 1. Instruments in which the wind vibrates in a hollow tube, like the flute, the single pipe, ordinary pipes of the organ, etc.
>
> 2. Instruments in which a single reed causes vibration, like the clarinet, bass clarinet, reed pipes of the organ, etc.
>
> 3. Instruments in which a double reed causes vibration, like the oboe and the double pipe.
>
> 4. Instruments in which elastic membranes are set in vibration a column of air (lips in a mouthpiece), like the trumpet, trombone, and tuba.

Most pipes have equidistant finger holes. The various musical scales and notes are produced by the size of the holes, the breath, the fingering, or some special device; as well as playing techniques that will be detailed in this chapter.

## 3.1 THE MAGIC NAY (END-BLOWN FLUTE)

Shown is a flute from tomb near pyramids - 4th Dynasty.

Nays are made from the reed plants which grow abundantly along the banks of the numerous irrigation canals in the Nile Valley. From this very simple plant, the Egyptians (then and now) were/are able to provide an incredible range of tones. No instrument had/has a more incorporeal sound, a sweeter sostenuto, or a more heartfelt vibrato.

The Egyptian (ancient and present) nay differs from the common present-day flute in two main ways:

1. The nay is made only of reed, and the flute is made of wood or metal.

2. The nay is end-blown, and the flute is stopped at one end and blown over a side hole.

There are also differences between the nay (end-blown flute) and the pipes, regarding the length, number, and locations of finger-holes; etc.

The sounds of the Egyptian nay are produced by blowing through a very small aperture of the lips against the edge of the orifice of the tube, and directing the wind into the tube. By opening and closing the finger holes, the resulting variation changes the length of air in the columns, providing the different pitches. The resulting sounds provide melodies—by steps and by leaps, brisk and longing, staccato, legato, and in tender pulsations and foamy cascades.

The Egyptian nay (end-blown flute) changed little in appearance over the course of the Egyptian history. It is one of the most popular instruments in Egypt today.

Nays are produced in seven different lengths, between 14.8" and 26.8" (37½ and 68 cm). The construction and measurement of the finger holes of today's nays (end-blown flutes) still adhere to the same principles as those of Ancient Egypt, as follows:

1. They are always cut from the upper part of the reed plant.

2. Each nay consists of nine joints/knuckles.

3. Each nay has six holes on the front and one hole on the back. The typical layout of the finger and thumb holes are shown below:

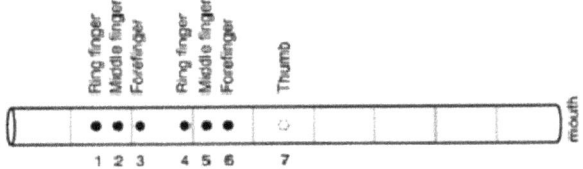

The Egyptian flute (nay) is considered a vertical flute.

The vertical-type flutes have/had greater musical possibilities than the whistle flutes. Being able to vary the angle of blowing against the edge, the player could give more expression to the tone.

Players of the nay (end-blown flute) direct the instrument (to a limited extent) to the right, left, and straight ahead, as shown herein. The players were/are able to accomplish endless intermediate values by driving or dropping the blowing air stream.

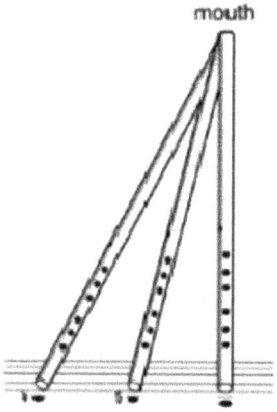

By blowing with more or less force, sounds are produced an octave higher or lower. Through the technique of over-blowing, the musician can play a range of more than three octaves.

The player requires considerable finesse. In order to achieve any desired tone, the player must control, coordinate, and manipulate several things: the strength and direction of his breath; the tension of his lips; the movement of his tongue; and the position of the lip and head, as well as opening or closing the finger holes in diverse combinations.

Since a single nay (end-blown flute) with a certain length can only provide a limited number of musical pitches, the Egyptian musicians (then and now) used/use a set of seven different lengths of nays in order to change the tonality and/or to change the pitch through increasing or decreasing the tones. A set of seven nays complement each other to provide a whole and complete range of very small notes in the compass of several octaves.

The player utilized/utilizes a set of seven lengths housed in a case, in order to obtain all tonal requirements. The seven lengths of the Egyptian nays (end-blown flutes) are: 26.8, 23.6, 21.3, 20.1, 17.5, 15.9, and 14.8 inches (68, 60, 54, 51, 44½, 40½, and 37½ cm).

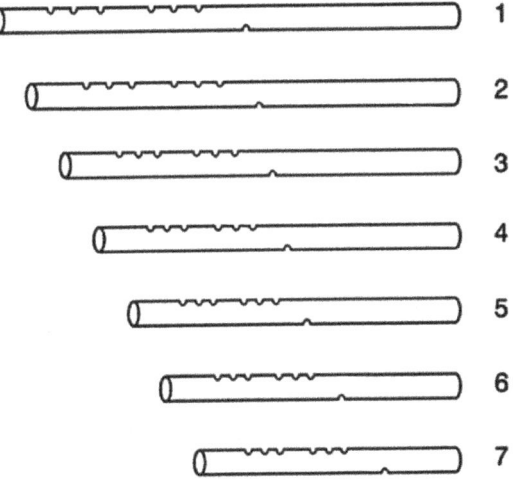

From the Middle Kingdom era [20th century BCE], Ancient Egyptian flutes from temples of Armant III give (according to C. Sachs) intervals (in cents) of 248 (11

Egyptian commas), 316 (14 commas), or 182 (4 commas), with an overall range of a natural Fifth of 702 cents (31 commas).

The measurements between the examined Ancient Egyptian nays' finger holes (not taking into account the various playing techniques) reveals that several tight-stepped scales were known, with intervals less than a ¼ tone (equivalent to two Egyptian musical commas).

Several of these Ancient Egyptian instruments are scattered in museums and private collections throughout the world. Some examples of found and/or depicted nays include:

- A slate palette [ca. 3200 BCE, now at Ashmolean Museum [at Oxford], depicts a number of animals. Among them is a jackal, playing the nay (end-blown flute).

- The tomb of Nencheftka, Saqqara [5th Dynasty—c. 2400 BCE, now in the Cairo Museum] depicts a nay player.

- Different lengthened nays (end-blown flutes) from Saqqara [now in the Cairo Museum, Cat. # 69815 and 69816].

- A relief from the tomb of Nekauhor at Saqqara [2390 BCE, now in the Metropolitan Museum of Art, New York].

- Representations in several tombs in Luxor (Thebes), during the 18th Dynasty.

The Egyptian nay was/is important for functions related to rebirth/renewal themes. The nay (flute) continues to maintain its mystical significance. The most common nay of the modern Egyptians is known as the Dervish nay because it is played by the mystical fellowship of Dervishes to accompany the singing and dancing members, during their mystical activities.

## 3.2 TRANSVERSE FLUTE

Ancient Egyptians were familiar with transverse flutes, which were/are blown from the side, and horizontally held.

The use of the transverse flute is present in Ancient Egyptian musical scenes since the 4th Dynasty [2575-2465 BCE], such as the above scene from a tomb near the Giza Pyramids.

Several other representations are found in Ancient Egyptian tombs, such as an illustration of an Egyptian transverse flute player [now at the Pelizaeus Museum Hildesheim].

The Ancient Egyptian instrument had an excellent mouthpiece which was used to evenly distribute the breath, and which also functioned as a wind chamber.

Some Ancient Egyptian transverse flutes made of bronze,

with the above-mentioned mouthpieces, are housed in the Museum of Napoli. Other similar flutes were found in southern Egypt, towards Meroe.

### 3.3 PAN FLUTE

Pan-pipes were/are a set of graduated tubes; generally seven in number, each resembling a simple vertical flute. Each pipe was/is stopped at the lower end and has no finger holes. They were all joined together to form a raft. The upper ends formed a horizontal line so the player could shift his mouth along them, according to the note required.

Pan-pipes, raft form

Numerous Ancient Egyptian vessels for consecrated oil or cosmetics were found to be shaped like pan flutes. They date back to the New Kingdom, which proves that such instruments were already in existence at that time.

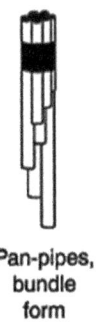

Pan-pipes, bundle form

Relatively few instruments of that kind were excavated. A well-preserved pan flute was unearthed in a Sobek temple at Fayoum. Another pan flute is illustrated in *Objects of Daily Use*, by Flinders Petrie.

## 3.4 SINGLE REED PIPE (CLARINET)

Pipes of all kinds were/are made from the reed plants which are abundant near the Egyptian irrigation canals.

The Egyptian single reed pipe (clarinet) contains a reed near the mouth that vibrates when one blows directly into the hole, through the pipe. The breath is directed, through a wooden or ivory beak, onto a sharp "lip" cut in the pipe itself.

The Egyptian single reed pipe was of equal antiquity with the nay (flute). It was a straight tube, without any increase at the mouthpiece. The reed pipes differ from the nay in construction, such as length, number of holes, etc.

There are two Egyptian single reed pipes [now in the British Museum] that are 9 and 15 inches (23 and 38 cm) long, and others [now in the collection at Leiden] that vary in length from 7 to 15 (18 to 38 cm) inches.

Pipes had/have equidistant finger holes. Some of the reed pipes have three holes; others four, as is the case with 14 Ancient Egyptian pipes presently at Leiden. In order to produce a musical scale, the performer must control the size of the hole, the breath, the fingering, or by other special playing techniques.

The ratio between the finger holes (without taking into account other playing techniques) yields the following intervals on Egyptian instruments, now at:

- The Leiden Museum [#475 and 477]—12:9:8:7:6 twelfths;
- Torino [#8] and Berlin [#20667]—12:11:10:9:8 twelfths;
- Torino [#12]—14:12:11:10:9:8:7 fourteenths;
- Torino [#11]—11:10:9:8:7:6 elevenths.

## 3.5 DOUBLE PIPES

Numerous Ancient Egyptian reed pipes and double pipes were recovered from tombs and are now scattered in museums all over the world. The double pipes in Ancient Egypt had different kinds; some having only one mouth hole and others having two; but placed near enough together as to enable the performer to blow upon both pipes at the same time. The mouthpiece of a pipe consists of a thin tube, closed at the upper end. A tongue is cut into the tube, and it vibrates in the player's mouth.

The pipes are either of equal length, or one is shorter than the other. They are blown simultaneously and played in unison. Sometimes one pipe has finger holes and the other does not. Sometimes one pipe served as a drone accompaniment, and its holes were stopped with wax. The Egyptians occasionally inserted little pegs or tubes into some of the finger holes to regulate the order of intervals or the mode in which they intended to perform.

As the placement of the finger holes (and hence the tones) do not completely correspond to one another, there are certain lingering effects, as well as sharper and more penetrating tones than is the case with ordinary instruments. This drone playing is confirmed from three facts: the peculiar arrangement of the players' fingers in Egyptian art works; the present practice in Egypt; and the excavation of a pipe with all except one finger hole stopped with wax.

Pipes with many finger holes were used for playing melodies, while others were used for the production of an accompanying tone similar to a bagpipe's drone. As such, the double pipe allows different playing types:

    1. alternate playing,
    2. octave playing,
    3. a melody with a "pedal" either below or above,

4. "Duet playing"; i.e. the simultaneous performance of two melodies, whether rhythmically distinct or allied.

The mystical Egyptian Sufi fraternity of the Dervishes specializes in playing the double pipes.

The following is an overview of the different types of double pipes of Ancient (and present-day) Egypt:

**a. Double Clarinet** is the common name for the instrument consisting of two pipes of equal length, parallel to each other and tied together. The pipes are made of the prolific reed plant.

Double clarinets are depicted on reliefs [from 2700 BCE], such as in the tomb of Nencheftka [5th Dynasty, Saqqara, now exhibited in Cairo Museum, Cat. #11533, shown herein], which shows a double clarinet made of two canes, equal in length and identically carved. This depictio is exactly like the *zummarah*—a popular Egyptian instrument used in folk music of today. The position of fingers and the posture while playing also coincide with the modern practice of music.

The ancient (and present-day) double clarinet of Egypt is made of two canes glued and tied alongside one another and provided with equidistant, and symmetrically arranged, finger holes (4, 5, or 6) in each cane. In the upper ends, smaller canes are inserted, out of which the beating tongue is cut by a three-sided slit. The player stops the corresponding holes of both tubes simultaneously with one finger; and as the holes, roughly cut into an uneven cane, produce slightly different pitches, the effect is a pulsating sound such as in the modern occidental organ stop, unda maris.

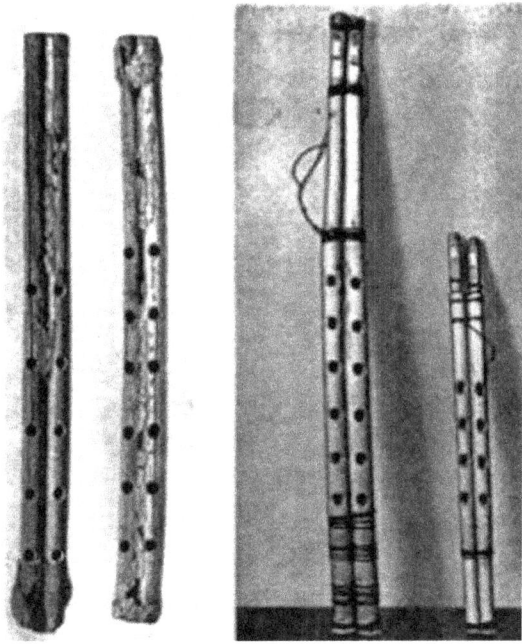

As in glass blowing, breathing is exclusively through the nose, while the mouth emits a constant blast of air. A different type of blowing is used for the modification of timbre and force, and the sound is emitted with unaltering strength and shrillness.

The Egyptian double clarinet comes in two variations, based on the style of mouthpiece:

1. The *zummarah*, which has its vibrating reed cut from the lower end of the mouthpiece. This version allows for articulation of high notes, obtained by holding the instrument in a horizontal position and over-blowing.

2. The *mashurah*, with the reed cut from the upper end. The instrument is held at a downwards-sloping angle, and as such, produces lower notes.

Some examples of found and/or depicted reed pipes are noted below:

- The double clarinet is depicted in Ancient Egyptian musical scenes since the Old Kingdom [4th Dynasty].

- A double clarinet in a relief from the tomb of Nekauhor [Saqqara, 5th Dynasty, now at the Metropolitan Museum of Art, New York].

• A double clarinet player is depicted in the tomb of Imery [Giza, Old Kingdom, 5th Dynasty]. The postures and techniques of playing, as well as the number of finger holes, are shown. One of these holes is seen at the forefinger of the widely stretched right hand of the player.

• A 12" (31 cm) long double clarinet from the New Kingdomera [now at the Cairo Museum, Cat. #69837 and 69838].

**b. Double Oboe** is the common name for the instrument consisting of two reed pipes of equal length in divergent positions. Each pipe has a reed that causes vibrations. The result is a type of polyphony with heterphonic expression.

There are many depictions in Ancient Egyptian tombs, detailing this instrument. Some show the player stopping a hole on each pipe with one finger stretched across.

Surviving oboes, since the Old Kingdom, were found in cases, each containing a set of different lengths—from 8 to 24 inches (20-60 cm). The number of holes ranges from 3 to 7 to 11.

Today's Egyptian players of oboes, like their ancestors, also possess several instruments, which are put together as a set in a case in order to satisfy all tonal requirements of their repertoire.

Some examples of found and/or depicted oboes include:

- A quiver-formed case, discovered near Dier elBakhit [Tomb No. 37, Luxor (Thebes), New Kingdom, now at the Cairo Museum, Cat #69836], comprised of six oboe pipes (three double oboes). The found case contained fragments of the mouthpiece; oboe "sheets" made of straw. In order to meet all tonal requirements of the performances, the player placed small wax lumps in the unneeded finger holes.

Several finger holes of these oboes still contain this filling, and a piece of wax was even found in a case.

• A double oboe [shown below] is depicted in the tomb of Nakht [Luxor (Thebes), dating from the 15th century BCE]. The instrument has several finger holes—some visible; others are covered by the musician's hands.

• A wall painting from an 18th Dynasty (1425-1375 BCE) tomb [Luxor (Thebes), now at the British Museum, #37948] shows the double oboe, which depicts the dark brown color of the oboe pipes separate from the light yellow mouthpiece made of straw.

In effect, oboes used to be blown with straw "sheets", as shown by excavated instruments.

**c. Arghool** is the name of the instrument consisting of a double clarinet with pipes of different lengths, parallel to each other and laced together. One pipe is much longer than the other. The longer pipe serves as a drone, providing a prolonged organ point. The shorter pipe provides the melody type.

One of the reed pipes of the *arghool* contains no finger holes at all (or, a number remarkably less than the melody reed).

The bourdon pipes are some yards/meters long and can, according to the player's discretion, be elongated by (mostly) two extensions, in order to turn from one mode to another. Adjectival extensions determine the size of the instrument (small, middle-sized, or huge instruments) as well as the number of finger holes (five, six, or seven).

As with the case of the double clarinet, there are two versions of arghool mouthpieces: the *zummarah* and the *mashurah*.

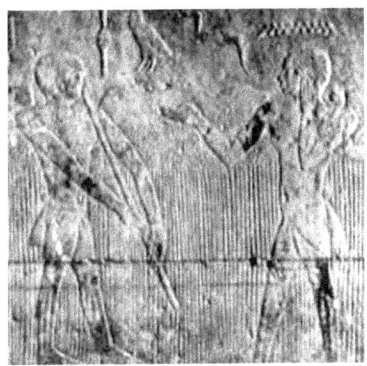

### d. Others

The principle and method of playing double pipes applies also to the bagpipe, whose prototypes date back to Ancient Egypt.

Ancient Egyptians have also developed and used the organ (in its pneumatic and hydraulic form).

## 3.6 THE TWIN HORNS/TRUMPETS

Horns/trumpets were known in Ancient Egypt since its very early times. Generally, trumpets in Ancient Egypt always appeared in pairs. With the typical two horns, one was sounded at dawn; the other at dusk.

Buq/buk is an Egyptian (not Arabic) word that means 'mouth'. It was out of the divine mouth (Re) that the divine sound (Thoth) came, with the harmonic series (over- and under-tone series). The more or less conical horn (*albuq*) has survived in the Spanish terms *alboque, alboquea,* or *albuquea*.

The Egyptian trumpet was straight, like the later Roman tuba or the present-day trumpet. Ancient Egypt had a variety of trumpets. They were generally 2 to 3 feet (60-90 cm) long, and were made of brass or bronze, with mouthpieces and flares or "bells" at the other end.

The horn/trumpet was not a "military" instrument. The sounds of the horns/trumpets were related to rebirth motifs—a transition from one stage to another. As such, they were/are utilized:

- Then and now, during funerary processions to "wake up" the deceased (resurrection). As such, it was attributed to Osiris, the principle of resurrection.

- To mark/announce both the new day (at dusk) and the end of the night (at dawn). There were two different horns for two different (but complementary) purposes. They were both used in temple rituals.

- To celebrate rebirth, as in the New Year celebration.

Some found and depicted trumpets include:

- A trumpet player in the Kagemni tomb [c. 2300 BCE, Saqqara].

- A wall painting from the tomb of Nebamon [Luxor (Thebes), Tomb 90, c. 1410 BCE] shows a trumpet player who precedes a funeral procession.

- Silver and golden (maybe copper) trumpets from the tomb of Tut-Ankh-Amen [1361-1352 BCE, now at the Cairo Museum, cat.#69850 and 69851]. The trumpets [shown herein] were found separate from one another.

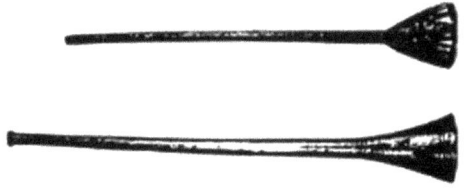

The silver trumpet measured 22.5" (57.1 cm), while the copper one was only 19.5" (49.5 cm) in length. Both ended with flares or "bells". The ratio between the lengths of the two trumpets is 8:9; the Perfect Tone.

- A trumpet blower of the Apet (New Year) procession is depicted in a relief from the temple of Luxor, from the time of Tut-Ankh-Amen [1361-1352 BCE].

>>> Several photographs in support of the text of this chapter are to be found in the digital edition of this book as published in PDF and E-book formats.

# 4

# Percussion Instruments

.Percussion instruments can be categorized under membrano- and non-membrano-phone instruments; i.e., whether or not a skin or parchment-type sheet is used.

## 4.1 MEMBRANO-PHONE INSTRUMENTS

### a. Drums

Ancient Egypt had a wealth and variety of drums of different shapes, sizes, and functions; some with skin on one or both sides. Some were struck with sticks; others with fingers and palms.

We are acquainted with three main kinds of Ancient Egyptian drum:

> **1. Cylindrical.** This kind of drum does not appear in any of the walls of tombs or temples (evidence that the variety of Ancient Egyptian instruments is not limited to the depicted musical scenes in tombs and temples). A few actual drums were found in Ancient Egyptian tombs. A drum [shown herein, now at the Berlin Museum] is 1½ ft. (46 cm) high and 2 ft. (61 cm) broad. Like other similar drums, it had cords for bracing it, and the cords could be tightened or slackened.

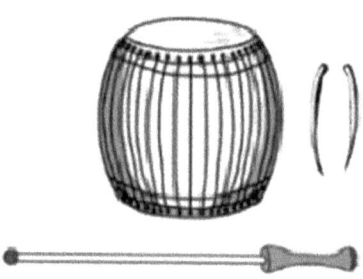

It was beaten with two slightly bent drumsticks. The Egyptians also had straight drumsticks with a handle and a knob at the end. Some of these are now in the Berlin Museum.

**2. Small hand drum**—elongated barrel-shape from 2 to 3 feet (61-91 cm) in length, covered with parchment at both ends. The performer was able to beat on both ends with his hands, fingers, or knuckles.

**3. Single skin drum,** which is a smaller type. This type was also rarely depicted in tombs. There are two kinds of this drum. The first kind is the earthen tabla/*darabukkah* (also called *goblet drum*). It is usually from 1½ ft. to 2 ft. (46 cm to 61 cm) long. The other kind is made of wood inlaid with mother-of-pearl and tortoise-shell, covered with a piece of fish's skin at the larger extremity and open at the smaller end, of about 15 inches (38 cm) in length.

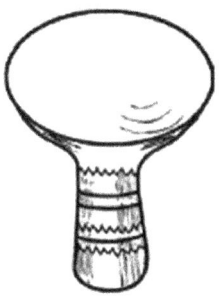

The membrane is struck with both hands. Drum playing with the bare hands, knuckles, and fingers has, in Egypt, reached perfection in technique, variety of timbre, and intricacy of rhythm. A good *tabla/ darabukkah* player, like a tambourine player, must have a command of the entire rhythmic pattern (timing—setting the tempo) repertoire.

The player produces the heavy principal beats, as with the frame drum, at the center; whereas light secondary beats are produced near the rim. Differentiating the sounds in this way, the drum player is able to present the rhythmic timing.

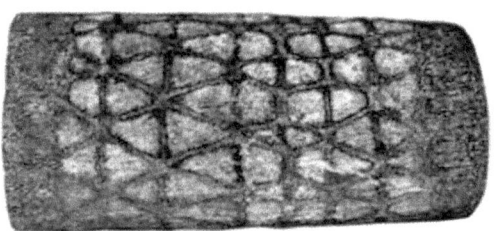

### b. Tambourines

The tambourine (riqq/tar) is a single-headed instrument with a diameter of approximately 8" (20 cm), covered with fish skin (or with a goat skin) membrane. The frame is mounted with ten pairs of cymbals set inside vertical pairs of "cymbal windows" that are cut out of the frame in a symmetrical arrangement. The tambourine is held in the left hand by the thumb and the fingers in such a manner that the fingers can also strike the rim of the frame. The right hand maneuvers at the center as well as at the edge of the membrane. These two positions correspond to a light drumbeat and a heavy one; and as such, they set the required rhythmic timing.

The *daff* (*duff*), like the riqq/tar, is a tambourine. This instrument, however, has a larger diameter—approximately 12" (30 cm)—and a shallower frame. It is not used to perform rhythmic timing (*wazn*) patterns.

Examples of Ancient Egyptian membrano-phone instruments include:

- A fragment from Ne-user-re's temple of the Sun, near Abusir [ca. 2700 BCE, now in the Munich museum], shows the top of a large drum.

- A 4,000 year old cylindrical drum [now in the Cairo Museum] was found in good condition in a tomb in Beni-Hasan. It is 25.6 inches (65 cm) long and 11.4 inches (29 cm) wide, and has a network of thongs with a tightening tourniquet to stretch the leather skins. Both eardrums were strongly tightened together in a crosswise position which pulled them firmly to one another.

- A number of drummers accompany the *Apet* Festival procession, depicted in the Luxor Temple, from the time of Tut-Ankh-Amen [1361-1352 BCE].

- A well preserved drum [dated from the 18th Dynasty, now at the Cairo Museum, Cat. #69355] has the same dimensions as the drum from Beni-Hasan's tomb [shown earlier, above], but the body of the drum is made of bronze.

- A squared drum is depicted on a wall painting in the tomb of Rekhmire [from Luxor (Thebes), Tomb 100, dated to the first half of the 15th century BCE].

- There are several other drums in many museums throughout the world [such as the Metropolitan Museum of Art in New York and the Louvre in Paris], which are tightened in the same manner as the one mentioned above at the Cairo Museum.

- Small frame drums (riqq/tar) of the New Kingdom were found. Most of them were circular, but some had four concave sides.

- Some specimens of Egyptian circular frame drums can be seen in more than one museum.

## 4.2 NON-MEMBRANO-PHONE (IDIOPHONE) INSTRUMENTS

### a. Percussion Sticks

Percussion sticks are considered to be a type of clapper. They have been recorded on Ancient Egyptian vases made before 3000 BCE, carefully drawn. Percussion sticks consist of two sticks; each held in a hand or both held in one hand and clapped against one another by the players.

Scenes of playing with percussion sticks are depicted in Ancient Egyptian tombs as a part of ritual dances during times of harvest. In an Ancient Egyptian tomb of about 2700 BCE, a representation of a file of farmers are shown, clapping sticks together as they advance in those long, easy strides typical of fertility rites in a ritual dance.

Similar presentations are found in other tombs of the Old Kingdom, such as a relief from the tomb of Neferirtenef, Saqqara [now in the Royal Museums of Art and of History, in Brussels].

Percussion sticks were also played during the pressing of grapes, as depicted in several tombs.

Currently, we know of four similar scenes. In each of them, we have two musicians who kneel opposite to one another, surrounded by an oval-shaped outline; each holding two pieces of wood in their hands. A clear example is depicted on a wall relief from the tomb of Mereruka (Saqqara, Old Kingdom). While the vintners press the grapes with their feet, two other men clap the rhythm with their sticks; one held in each hand.

**b. Clappers**

Ancient Egyptian clappers were used in all types of occasions. Clappers were/are frequently used to regulate music and the dance. They varied slightly in form. Some were made of wood, bone, ivory, or shells; others of brass (or some sonorous metal). Some have a straight handle, surmounted by a head or other ornamental device. Sometimes the handle is slightly curved and double, with two heads at the upper extremity. Clappers' heads were carved in the shape of animal presentations, falcon heads, bearded men, lotus flowers, gazelles, cow heads. Many are decorated with the head of Hathor. Hundreds of such clappers were found in Ancient Egyptian tombs.

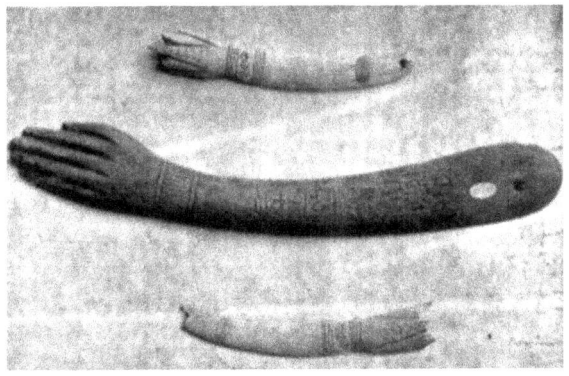

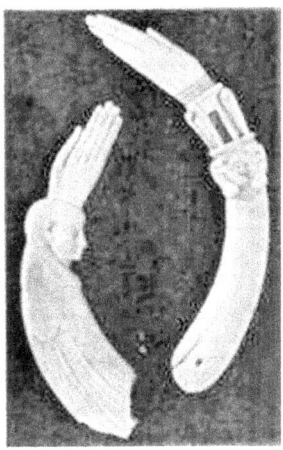

The performer held a clapper in each hand, and the sound depended on their size and material of which they were made. Sample representations include:

- Ivory clappers, from the 1st or 2nd Dynasty [now in the Cairo Museum, cat. #69457 and 69250].

- A pair of ivory clappers shaped like human hands, dating back to the 18th Dynasty [now in the Metropolitan Museum in New York].

- Two ivory clappers [now in the Cairo Museum, cat. #69234 and 69235].

- Straight ivory clappers in hand form [now in the Cairo Museum, cat. #69206].

## c. Sistrums/Sistra

The Ancient Egyptian sistrum was the sacred instrument par excellence, and belonged to the service of the temple.

It generally had 3 to 4 bars, and the whole instrument was from 8 to 16 or 18 inches (20, 40, 47 cm) in length, made entirely of brass or bronze. It was sometimes inlaid with silver or gilt; or otherwise ornamented. It was held upright and shaken, the rings moving to and fro upon the bars. The sistrum's bars were frequently made to imitate the asp, or were simply bent at each end to secure them.

It was so great a privilege to hold the sacred sistrum in the temple that it was given to queens and to those noble ladies who had the distinguished title of Women of Amun, who were devoted to the service of the deity.

Numerous representations of sistra were depicted throughout Egypt's dynastic history. A large number of Ancient Egyptian sistra were found, and are now in museums throughout the world.

### d. Cymbals

Egyptian cymbals were made of brass, or of silver and brass mixed. They varied in diameter from 5½ to 7 inches (14-18 cm) and were shaped just like modern instruments, even to the saucer-like depression in the middle.

Numerous cymbals were found buried in Ancient Egyptian tombs and are now scattered in museums throughout the world. The specimens preserved [in the Metropolitan Museum of Art in New York] are of two different sizes: 5 and 7 inches (12 and 18 cm) in diameter.

### e. Castanets

Tiny fingertip pairs of cymbals also were in use in Ancient Egypt. In later ages, these were carried by Egyptian immigrants to Spain, where they became known as castanets because they were made of chestnut (castaña).

These small-type cymbals, 2" to 3" (5-7.5 cm) in diameter, are played between thumb and middle finger up to this day. Castanets—called crotala—are used in pairs, and are struck together while dancing. The term castanets is used here in the narrower sense of clappers, the striking faces of which are hollowed out to give a fuller resonance.

Egyptian castanets existed in two forms: 1) shaped something like a very small wooden boot, cut in half, lengthwise, and grooved in the leg part, while the tapering foot part served as a handle; and 2) nearly the shape of modern Spanish castañuelas, but less flat. They looked like the chestnut, castaña, for which it was named.

Numerous Egyptian castanets were found in Ancient Egyptian tombs, and are now scattered throughout the museums and private collections worldwide.

The religious significance of castanets is shown in the musical scene of four musicians with castanets, depicted in the Apet procession at the Luxor Temple from the time of Tut-Ankh-Amen [c. 1360 BCE].

**f. Bells (Chimes)**

Ancient Egyptian bells of various kinds were found, carefully wrapped in cloth before they were placed in the tombs. A large number of these bells are now housed at the Egyptian Museum of Cairo. The sounds of some of them were tested, and it was proven that they have quite an extensive range of sound and tone pitches. They varied in weight in order to provide the various musical ratios of 9:8 for a whole note, 3:2 for the Fifth, and so on.

Bells were made mainly of bronze, but were also occasionally made of gold or silver. They came in different forms. Some have the form of bells with a jagged mouth, which is to represent a flower calyx, among a whole line of other types.

Having a large number of Ancient Egyptian bell molds [now in the Cairo Museum, Cat. #32315a, b] provides good evidence of the metal founding in Ancient Egypt

The influx hole for the liquid metal can be clearly seen.

The chemical analysis of the typical Ancient Egyptian bell was found to be 82.4% copper, 16.4% tin, and 1.2% lead.

Bells had/have a religious and functional significance in Egypt. Bells were worn by the temple priests during temple rituals. Bells were also used in those Ancient Egyptian festivals related to Osiris.

Bells are utilized as amulets, to protect people against evil spirits. Bells are suspended at the door to be rung by entering persons not to warn the owner of their arrival; but to protect the house and the caller against demons who lurk under the threshold.

Some other representations of Ancient Egyptian bells include:

- Animals with bells on a pre-dynastic vase, Negadah I Period.

- Fifteen bells are now present in the British Museum.

- Small bells from the New Kingdom era [now in the Cairo Museum, cat. #69594].

- Scenes of the inner inner part of the temple of Het-Heru (Hathor) in Dendera depict the priests wearing pieces of jewelry formed as bells, attached to their outfits at their foot bangles or at their sandals. Again, the true sense is that the little bell is an amulet whose function is to avert evil forces which protect the priests in the presence of deities.

- Many Ancient Egyptian necklaces of gold and silver consist of bell shapes, as shown in several museums.

**g. Xylophone and Glockenspiel**

An Egyptian instrument is represented as a companion to the lyre, in an Ancient Egyptian tomb. The instrument consists of a series of metallic bars, or of wooden slabs, arranged according to a certain order of intervals. It appears to be a kind of dulcimer. Or, even more likely, it may be a harmonicon.

## 4.3 HUMAN PARTS (HANDS, FINGERS, THIGHS, FEET, ETC.)

Rhythmic clapping of two groups of men and women from the tomb of Dhutmos (Tomb 342), Ta-Apet (Thebes) [18th Dynasty, now in the British Museum]

The Egyptian clapping with hands and stamping with feet turned, at an early time, into a finely-graded, dynamic and varied means of expression; and thus acquired an additional significance in Egypt, where it turned into a high art in their culture of music.

Egyptian clapping, foot-stamping, and finger snapping consisted of rhythmic beats (whether simple or complicated rhythms) which were tonally nuanced and dynamically well-balanced. The tonal differences were produced in such a manner that clapping used to take place as in Spain with palmas sordas or with palmas brillantes; i.e. with hollow or flat hands. In addition, and since primeval times, all possible other forms of body beats existed.

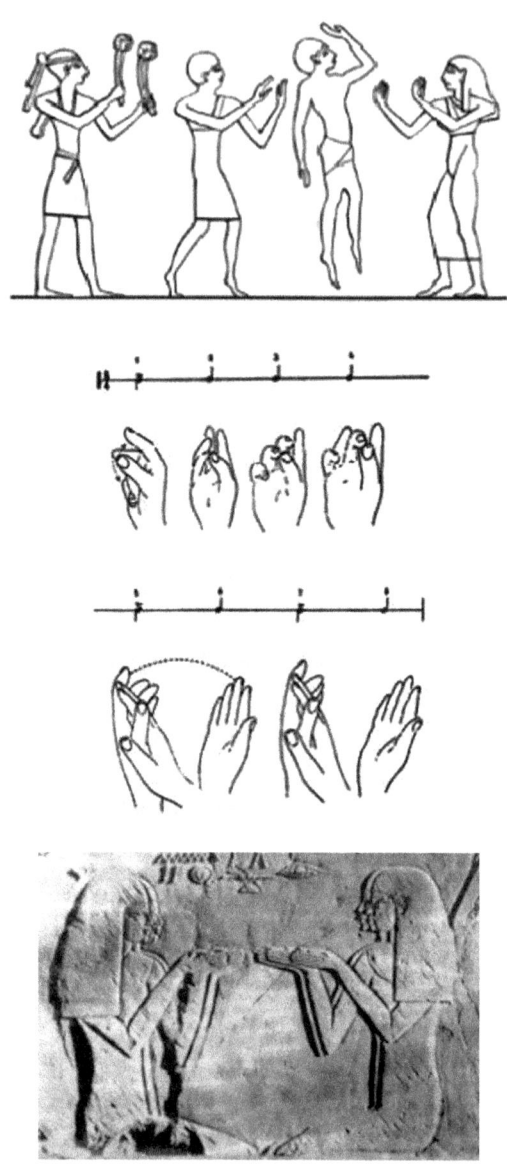

Hand-clapping of two groups [as shown above] can be between men and women or two groups of men or two groups of women. Two rhythmic accompanying patterns are played (say, 12 beats and 8 beats for the first and second groups). The hand-clapping marks the fundamental rhythmic beats until a rhythmic structure of a particular density is created by the interplay of clapping patterns performed by the two groups.

Two groups of women are shown in rhythmic hand-clapping in the Sed Festival, tomb of Kheruef, Luxor (Thebes), 18th Dynasty (15th century BCE).

>>> Several photographs in support of the text of this chapter are to be found in the digital edition of this book as published in PDF and E-book formats.

# 5

# The Musical Performance

## 5.1 THE HARMONIC MERIT HAND

Merit is the name of an Ancient Egyptian netert (goddess) who was considered to be the personification of music.

Merit's major function was to establish cosmic order by means of her gestures; and, as such, Merit is the cosmic conductor/maestro who manages the notes and the flow of musical performances.

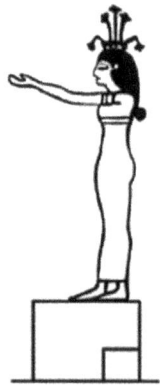

This understanding of the role of the hand in Ancient Egypt made Plato define music itself as *"the art of guiding the singers of a chorale"*. The Greeks have ascribed their hand waving signs to the Ancient Egyptian practice of music.

The hand of Merit is the universal symbol of action. Musically, the fingers control the sound emitted from musical instruments. How you place the fingers determines the tones. Therefore, fingers are the most logical way to express, write, and instruct music.

In Ancient (like present-day) Egypt, tones, strings, scales, and melodies are all related and are therefore expressed by a particular finger, *asba* (plural: *asabi*). In Egypt (Ancient and Baladi), this conventional "finger movement" mode was all that was needed to identify the different modes. In early years of the post-Islam era (after 640 CE), Arabicized countries used the same Egyptian finger expressions. After a few centuries, they began using another term, *maqam*, for a mode.

Ancient Egyptian tombs and temples yield several series of choreographic, rhythmic and melodic hand signs that correspond to certain signs of chironomids. The tones are presented by different positions of the arms and fingers (forefinger against the thumb, the stretched-out hand, etc.), resulting in an absolute correspondence between tonal steps of the Ancient Egyptian musical system and hand signals.

The chironomid presided over the musical ensemble and, by a range of gestures, determined the pitch and intervals upon which the musicians based their performance. The details of this examination are reported in a special study [H. Hickmann, *The Chironomy in Ancient Egypt*, Magazine of Egyptian Language and the Antique 83, 2, 1958.].

Symphonic and polyphonic variations are depicted in musical scenes of Ancient Egyptian buildings from the Old Kingdom (4500 years ago), which include a director to guide the total ensemble by means of visible gestures. One or more chironomids were depicted to signify the type of performance. It must be noted that depicting more than one chironomid for one instrument is symbolic of the action intended, in Ancient Egyptian artistic representation. Egyptian chironomids guided the musicians in basically three different ways, to provide single, double, and triple tonalities, as follows:

1. The chironomids are indicating identical hand signs,

thus the musician(s) is/are playing in unison.

2. The chironomids are indicating different hand signs; thus the musicians are playing a chord. The following are two examples:

> a. In the tomb of Ti [Saqqara, Old Kingdom], we have two illustrated chironomids giving different hand signals for a single instrument (harp) representing two different sounds; i.e. portraying an example of polyphony.

This depiction of two chironomids is indicative of double tonality, which could be either consecutive or simultaneous.

b. Playing a chord with three different tones is depicted [shown below] in Nencheftka's tomb [5$^{th}$ Dynasty, Saqqara, now in Cairo Museum]. Three different hand signals are shown by the depicted chironomids.

Another example of polyphony composed of three different tones is presented in a musical scene from a relief from the tomb of Nekauhor [Saqqara, 5$^{th}$ Dynasty, presently at the Metropolitan Museum of Art, New York].

## 5.2 THE WRITTEN SOUNDS

The Ancient Egyptians were extremely literal people who documented all aspects of their civilization in written form. Therefore, it should not come as a surprise that they also wrote musical sounds as they did their spoken sounds (language). For the Ancient Egyptians, music and language are two sides of the same coin. The written symbols (letters) are sonic pictures; i.e. each spoken letter has a specific vibration (pitch), just like the musical alphabet.

The Ancient Egyptian language is ideal for musical writing because its symbols (letters) can be written in any direction; and therefore their sequence can be inverted like a scale: up-down, right-left, or vice-versa.

Plato acknowledged that the Ancient Egyptians notated their musical tunes, in his *Laws* [656-7]:

> "...*postures and tunes that are harmonically pleasing. These they [the Egyptians] prescribed in detail and posted up in the temples*..."

All early Greek and Roman writers affirmed that there were basically two forms of Ancient Egyptian writings—pictorial and alphabetical. There were different modes of the alphabetical writings, depending on the subject matter as well as the purpose of writing. We will focus our attention here on the forms associated with music and vocal musical themes: poetry, chanting, singing, etc.

François Joseph Fétis, an accomplished musicologist, discovered the roots of the Greeks' notation symbols to be the demotic form of the Ancient Egyptian writing.

F. J. Fétis states in his *Biographie Universelle des Musiciens et Bibliographie Générale de la Musique* [Bruxelles, 1837, tome I, p. lxxi.],

> "*I have not the least doubt, that this musical notation*

> *[used in ecclesiastical music by the modern Greeks] belonged to ancient Egypt. I have in support of my opinion the resemblance borne by the signs in this notation, erroneously attributed to St. John of Damascus, to those of the demotic, or popular characters of the ancient Egyptians..."*

M. Fétis continued by pointing out the resemblance existing between numerous symbols accredited to the Greeks to determine the duration of notes and certain characters of the Egyptian demotic symbols in a lengthy and detailed analysis [read more of the portion of the English translation of M. Fétis' text in Carl Engel's book, T*he Music of the Most Ancient Nations*, pages 271-2]. M. Fétis did not hesitate to conclude:

> *"After this detailed analysis of the system of notation employed in the music of the Greek Church, and after comparing its signs with those of the demotic character in use among the Egyptians, can we for a moment doubt that the invention of this notation is to be ascribed to that ancient people [the Egyptians], and not to St. John of Damascus..."*

M. Fétis's detailed analysis and conclusion proves without the shadow of any doubt that the Greeks borrowed the musical notation of the Egyptian demotic symbols.

Another musicologist – namely, Charles Burney [see bibliography] – noted that an inventory of available notations shows that the Ancients utilized more than 120 different characters for sound only. When taking into account the time (or tempo) variation as it relates to the different modes and genera, the sound characters were multiplied to more than 1620. Burney described this huge number as consisting mostly of lines, curves, hooks, right and acute angles, and other simple figures placed in varied positions; a form of what he described as *"mutilated foreign alphabet"*. The symbols of the so-called *"mutilated foreign alphabet"* are actually Ancient Egyptian demotic symbols, as noted by M. Fétis.

Unlike the present-day Western notation system that is comprised of cumbersome abstracts that must be memorized without thinking, it was, however, easier to learn and follow the Ancient Egyptian notation system, because it was consistent with their language.

A detailed analysis of the musical written forms in Ancient Egypt is to be found in the book *The Enduring Ancient Egyptian Musical System* by Moustafa Gadalla.

## 5.3 THE RHYTHMIC TIMING

As testified by Plato (*Philebus* 18-b, c, d), the Ancient Egyptians identified three elements that constitute an orderly flow of sound (regular pitch, noise, and muting). These three categories enable us to identify the duration of each sound, as well as the rest time (silence) between consecutive sounds.

Music, like language, is read in pattern; not individual units – i.e., we read words; not letters. Understanding music/words/phrases depends upon sensation and memory; for we must not only feel sounds at the instant they strike the instrument, but must remember those that had been struck before, in order to be able to compare them together. The time element involved in separating consecutive tones is the organizing factor in hearing, feeling, and comprehending the intent of music or spoken words/phrases.

The emotional effect of music depends largely upon the type of rhythm that it employs. Rhythm means flow: a movement that surges and recedes in intensity. The flow of rhythm assumes many forms in music. Much of the color and personality of music comes from its rhythm. This may be the contrast of strong and weak impulses, long and short note values, low and high pitch, slow or fast, and even or uneven, with accents frequent or infrequent. Combinations of these elements give rhythm its character.

Maintaining a specific rhythm was/is very critical, since the strict union of poetry and music among the Ancient and Baladi Egyptians seems to have been almost inseparable. As such, any deviation from the specified time or rhythm not only destroyed the beauty of the poetry, but sometimes even the meaning of the words from which it was composed. A change in vowel pronunciation makes it a different sound—a different vowel—and hence, a different word.

Beating time in music is quite important, because if a musician (not a percussionist) falls out of time, the music sounds off, and the ear tends to stop listening and to drift. Beat is a constant pulsation. It acts as a ruler by which we can measure the duration of a note and the time between notes. Time beating could be accomplished by any of the following ways:

    1. Musicians learn to keep time quietly with the aid

of onomatopoeic syllables. The correspondence between syllables and musical notes makes this method of keeping time very natural. Singing to/with music follows the same pattern, and can be accomplished in two ways: 1) by using certain syllables for the duration of the note, and/or for time in between notes; 2) through an even or alternate recurrence of numbers, by counting to oneself.

Usually, two sizes of syllables are utilized: short and long (i.e. a long/longer vowel, at a ratio of 2:1). These two basic elements are used in numerous variations for variable meters (the sequence of beats and rests contained in each time segment).

2. Foot beating is depicted in Ancient Egyptian musical scenes[shown in far right, below], as a method of keeping time.

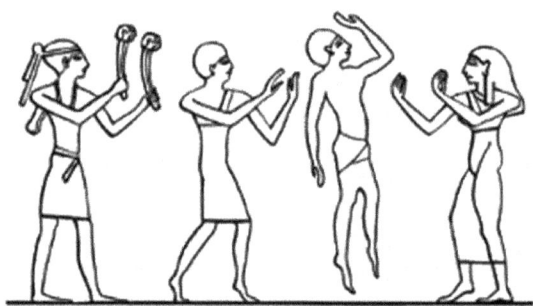

3. In many musical representations in Ancient Egyptian buildings, musicians are accompanied by a person clapping, or using clappers, to keep the musicians in time.

4. The Egyptians utilized/utilize the drum patterns of small hand drums, the goblet drum (tabla/

darabukkah), the frame drum (riqq or tar), or the pair of kettle drums (naqqarat) to regulate the time.

5. Classical Egyptian practices had **two kinds of beats working in combination; silent and audib**le:

> • **Silent gestures** were used in Ancient Egypt, in various ways, by giving signals such as: lifting the forearm, turning the palm either up or down, and stretching or doubling up the fingers; one hand held partly out with thumb and forefinger forming a circle and other fingers held stiffly, while the other hand is placed on the ear or on the knee in a relaxed position, with the palm upward or downward. The thumb may be up, or bent against the forefinger.

[A few examples of time-beating, as shown in tombs in Sakkara from the Old Kingdom.]

In performing these movements, the hands alternated from member to member between the right hand, the left hand, and both hands.

The fingers, too, alternated. In duple time, the four parts of a period were denoted by pointing first with the small finger and successively adding the ring finger, the middle finger, and the index finger.

- **Audible beats** were also provided by snapping the fingers; slapping (as the thigh) with the right hand or with the left hand; or slapping with both hands.

In the tomb of Amenemhet at Luxor (Thebes), dated c. 1500 BCE, a conductor is depicted standing before and facing the performers, pounding time with her right heel and snapping both her thumbs and her forefingers.

## 5.4 MOODS AND MODES

We all recognize that certain musical modes make us happy, while others make us sad. The emotional power of different musical modes puts us in different moods, such as: exuberance, intoxication, exaltation, religious devotion, love, playfulness, whimsicality, reflectiveness, seriousness, patriotism, sadness, longing, mournfulness, passion, serenity, calmness, joyfulness, despair, frenzied melancholy, mysticism, agitation, etc.

It is therefore that the composition of a melody/mode must follow certain design criteria in order to meet the desired objective. This fact was first known and implemented in Ancient Egypt.

In the 4th century BCE, Plato recommended that the Ideal State be erected upon the foundation of music—a well-established system based on a theory of the ethos of music; a theory of the psycho-physiological effects of music on the State and on man. Plato's recommendation was the adoption of Ancient Egypt's system and practices, as stated in Plato's Collected Dialogues, in *Laws II* [656c–657c]:

*ATHENIAN: Then is it conceivable that anywhere*

where there are, or may hereafter be, sound laws in force touching this educative-playful function of the Muses, <u>men of poetic gifts should be free to take whatever in the way of rhythm, melody, or diction tickles the composer's fancy in the act of composition and teach it through the choirs</u> to the boys and lads of a law-respecting society, leaving it to chance whether the result prove virtue or vice?

CLINIAS: To be sure, that does not sound rational decidedly not.

ATHENIAN: And yet <u>this is precisely what they are actually left free to do, I may say, in every community with the exception of Egypt</u>.

CLINIAS: And in Egypt itself, now—pray how has the law regulated the matter there?

ATHENIAN: The mere report will surprise you. That nation, it would seem, long enough ago <u>recognized the truth we are now affirming, that poses and melodies must be good</u>, if they are to be habitually practiced by the youthful generation of citizens. So <u>they drew up the inventory of all the standard types, and consecrated specimens of them in their temples</u>.

. . .

ATHENIAN: . . .in this matter of music in Egypt, it is a fact, and a thought-provoking fact, <u>that it has actually proved possible, in such a sphere, to canonize melodies which exhibit an intrinsic rightness permanently by law</u>. . . So, as I was saying before, if we can *but detect the intrinsically right in such matters, in whatever degree, we should reduce them to law and system without misgiving, since the appeal to feeling which shows itself in the perpetual craving for novel musical sensation can, after all, do comparatively little to corrupt choric art, once it has been consecrated, by deriding it as out of fashion. <u>In Egypt, at any rate, its corrupting influence appears to have been nowise potent, but very much the reverse.</u>*

*CLINIAS: That seems to be the state of the case from your present account.*

*ATHENIAN: Then may <u>we say boldly that the right way to employ music and the recreations of the choric art is on some such lines as these?</u>When we believe things are going well with us, we feel delight, and, conversely, when we feel delight we believe things are well with us.*

The above scripts from Plato's Collected Dialogues show how the Greeks considered Ancient Egypt to be the sole source of their Ideal Laws, as related to music (among other things). The Greek text above admits the following:

1. Only Egypt had sound laws that govern melodies and poses.

2. Only Egypt had an inventory of well-designed standard type modes/melodies and the regulations by which they are performed—time, place, and occasion.

3. Only Egypt had practiced their prescribed Ideal Laws for music, dance, poetry, etc.

For more information about the theory, fundamentals, and musical practice of the Ancient (and present-day Baladi) Egyptians, read *The Enduring Ancient Egyptian Musical System* by Moustafa Gadalla.

>>> Several photographs in support of the text of this chapter are to be found in the digital edition of this book as published in PDF and E-book formats.

1

# GLOSSARY

**Baladi** – see *Standards and Terminology* at the beginning of the book.

**BCE** – **B**efore **C**ommon **E**ra. Also noted in other references as BC.

**beat** – a constant pulsation. It acts as a ruler by which we can measure time.

**buk-nunu** – an Ancient Egyptian musical unit equal to 7.55 cents, which is 1/3 of a comma.

**CE** – **C**ommon **E**ra. Also noted in other references as AD.

**cent** – a standard unit for measuring musical intervals. An octave is equal to 1,200 cents.

**chironomid** – one who gestures with his/her hands—a maestro/conductor.

**chironomy** – the art of conducting or representing music by gestures of the fingers, hand(s), and/or arm(s).

**chord** – a combination of three or more tones sounded together in harmony.

**comma** – an Ancient Egyptian musical unit, equal to 22.64 cents.

**diatonic** – a scale consisting of 5 whole tones and 2 semitones. **enharmonic** – designating a ¼ step/note or less.

**ethos** – the expression of a mode that is connected to its structure. Describes the ethical power or moral force of a mode and its ability to influence the development of character and attitudes in the listener.

**Fifth** – can mean either: 1) the fifth tone of an ascending diatonic scale, or a tone four degrees above or below any given tone in such a scale—dominant. 2) the interval between two such tones, or a combination of them.

**Fourth** – can mean either: 1) the fourth tone of an ascending diatonic scale, or a tone three degrees above or below any given tone in such a scale—subdominant. 2) the interval between two such tones, or a combination of them.

**fret** – narrow, lateral ridges fixed across the finger board of a stringed instrument, such as a guitar, etc., to guide the fingering.

**halftone** – see **semitone**.

**heptatonic** – consists of seven (hepta) tones.

**interval** – can mean either: 1) the ratio of the number of vibrations between two different tones. 2) The distance separating two consecutive musical notes. [Also see **tone** and **semitone**.]

**meter** – succession of equal beats characterized by the periodic return of a strong beat.

**mode** – a rhythmical system consisting of its own unique combination of tones and rhythms, in order to provide specific influence on the listener. [Also see **ethos**.]

**neter/netert** – a divine principle/function/attribute of the One Great God. (Incorrectly translated as god/goddess).

**notes** – in Western musical terms, the letters A (La) to G (Sol) are used to designate notes.

**onomatopoeic** – the naming of a thing or action by a vocal imitation of sound associated with it (ex: hiss).

**pentatonic** – a scale consisting of five tones—three of which are whole-tones, and two semitones—like that of the black keys on a keyboard.

**perfect** – the name given to certain intervals—the Fourth, Fifth, and Octave. The term is applied to these intervals in their natural sounds (not "tempered").

**pitch** – the position of a tone in a musical scale, determined by the frequency of vibration and measured by cycles per second.

**polyphony** – the simultaneous sounding of different notes; the sounding of two or more different melodies simultaneously.

**scale** – any series of eight tones to the octave, arranged in a step-by-step rising or falling of pitch, which consists of a given pattern of intervals (the differences of pitch between notes).

**semitone** – the intervals between B (Si) and C (Do), and between E (Mi) and F (Fa). [Also see **tone**.]

**step** – interval of sound.

**tetrachord** – a series of four tones comprising a total interval of a Perfect Fourth; half an octave.

**timbre** – the quality or color of the sound invoked. It distinguishes one voice or instrument from another.

**tone** – the combination of pitch, intensity (loudness) and quality (timbre). The interval between each of the notes is a tone, except between B (Si) and C (Do) and between E (Mi) and F (Fa), where the interval is a semitone in each case.

**tonality** – the relationship between musical sounds or tones, taking into account their vibratory relationships and their appreciation by the ear. A systematic musical structure.

**unison** – the same sound, produced by two or more instruments or voices.

2

# SELECTED BIBLIOGRAPHY

Burney, Charles. *A General History of Music*, 2 volumes. New York, 1935.

Engel, Carl. *The Music of The Most Ancient Nations*. London, 1929.

Erlanger, Baron Rodolphe. *La Musique Arabe*. Paris, 1930.

Erman, Adolf. *Life in Ancient Egypt*. New York, 1971.

Farmer, H.G. *The Sources of Arabian Music*. Leiden, 1965.

Farmer, H.G. *Historical Facts for the Arabian Music Influence*. New York, 1971.

Fétis, François Joseph. *Biographie Universelle des Musiciens et Bibliographie Générale de la Musique*. (*Universal Biography of Musicians*). Bruxelles, 1837.

Gadalla, Moustafa. *Egyptian Cosmology: The Animated Universe*. USA, 2001.

Gadalla, Moustafa. *Egyptian Harmony: The Visual Music.* USA, 2000.

Gadalla, Moustafa. *Egyptian Rhythm: The Heavenly Melodies.* USA, 2002.

Haïk-Vantoura, Suzanne. *The Music of the Bible Revealed.* Tr. by Dennis Weber/Ed. by John Wheeler. Berkeley, CA, 1991.

Herodotus. *The Histories.* Tr. By Aubrey DeSelincourt. London, 1996.

Hickmann, Hans. *Musikgeschichte in Bildern: Ägypten.* Leipzig, Germany, 1961.

Hickmann, Hans. *Orientalische Musik.* Leiden, 1970.

Levy, Ernst and Siegmund LeVarie. *Music Morphology – A discourse and dictionary.* Kent, Ohio, USA, 1983.

Levy, Ernst and Siegmund LeVarie. *Tone: A Study in Musical Acoustics.* Kent, Ohio, USA, 1980.

Manniche, Lise. *Music and Musicians in Ancient Egypt.* London, 1991.

Plato. *The Collected Dialogues of Plato including the Letters.* Edited by E. Hamilton & H. Cairns. New York, USA, 1961.

Polin, Claire C. J. *Music of the Ancient Near East.* New York, 1954.

Sachs, Curt. *The History of Musical Instruments.* New York, 1940.

Sachs, Curt. *The Rise of Music in the Ancient World.* New York, 1943.

Sachs, Curt. *The Wellsprings of Music.* The Hague, Holland, 1962.

Siculus, *Diodorus*. Vol 1. Tr. by C.H. Oldfather. London, 1964.

Stanford, C.V. and Forsyth, Cecil. *A History of Music*. New York, 1925.

Touma, H.H. *The Music of the Arabs*. Portland, Oregon, USA, 1996.

Wilkinson, J. Gardner. *The Ancient Egyptians: Their Life and Customs*. London, 1988.

Numerous references in Arabic language.

# 3

# SOURCES AND NOTES

My references to the sources are listed in the previous section, Selected Bibliography. They are only referred to for facts, events, and dates; not for their interpretations of such information.

It should be noted that if a reference is made to one of the author Moustafa Gadalla's books, that each of his books contain appendices for its own extensive bibliography as well as detailed Sources and Notes.

## Chapter 1: The Wealth of Instruments

**Pitches and Scales:** Sachs (History of Musical Instruments, Rise of Music), Hickmann (Musikgeschichte in Bildern: Ägypten, Orientalische Musik)

**Musicians in Ancient Egypt:** Hickmann (Musikgeschichte in Bildern: Ägypten, Orientalische Musik), Wilkinson, Gadalla (Historical Deception, Egyptian Cosmology), Burney, Diodorus, Blackman

**Musical Orchestra:** Wilkinson, Hickmann (Musikgeschichte in Bildern: Ägypten, Orientalische Musik)

**Other Items:** Gadalla (Egyptian Cosmology, Egyptian Harmony), Herodotus, Plato, Blackman, Gadalla as a native Egyptian

## Chapter 2: Stringed Instruments

**Lyres:** Polin, Engel, Wilkinson, Hickmann (Musikgeschichte in Bildern: Ägypten)

**Lyres–Compass:** Sachs (History of Musical Instruments), Hickmann (Orientalische Musik, Musikgeschichte in Bildern: Ägypten)

**Tri-gonon/Ka-Nun:** Hickmann (Orientalische Musik), Sachs (History of Musical Instruments), Egyptian literature in Arabic

**Harps:** Wilkinson, Polin, Hickmann (Musikgeschichte in Bildern: Ägypten) [Specific examples in tombs]

**Harp playing techniques:** Hickmann (Musikgeschichte in Bildern: Ägypten), Sachs (Rise of Music)

**Capacity of Harps:** Manniche, Engel, Sachs (History of Musical Instruments), Burney

**Neck Instruments:** Engel, Sachs (History of Musical Instruments), Farmer [Arabized Era], Erlanger [Arabized Era], Hickmann (Orientalische Musik, Musikgeschichte in Bildern: Ägypten), Manniche, Polin, Wilkinson

**Tuning pegs:** Engel, Polin

**2-strings:** Burney (Compass), Hickmann (Musikgeschichte in Bildern: Ägypten) [Samples in tombs]

**3-strings:** Engel, Manniche

**4-strings:** Engel

**Short-neck:** Hickmann (Musikgeschichte in Bildern: Ägypten), Manniche

**Egyptian Guitars:** Hickmann (Musikgeschichte in Bildern: Ägypten), Engel, Wilkinson

**Various examples in Ancient Egyptian tombs:** Hickmann (Musikgeschichte in Bildern: Ägypten), Engel, Manniche

**Bowed instruments:** Hickmann (Musikgeschichte in Bildern: Ägypten), Touma, Wilkinson

## Chapter 3: Wind Instruments

**Nay:** Polin, Hickmann (Musikgeschichte in Bildern: Ägypten), Egyptian literature in Arabic, Sachs (History of Musical Instruments), Wilkinson, Engel

**Playing Techniques:** Engel, Sachs (Wellspring), Sachs (History of Musical Instruments), Hickmann (Orientalische Musik)

**Examples in tombs:** Hickmann (Musikgeschichte in Bildern: Ägypten)

**Transverse Flute:** Hickmann (Musikgeschichte in Bildern: Ägypten), Polin, Wilkinson, Sachs (History of Musical Instruments)

**Pan Flute:** Sachs (History of Musical Instruments), Hickmann (Musikgeschichte in Bildern: Ägypten)

**Single Pipe:** Wilkinson, Gadalla (Egyptian Rhythm)

**Partial analysis of pipes in different museums:** Sachs (Rise of Music)

**Double Pipes:** Stanford/Forsyth, Wilkinson, Hickmann (Musikgeschichte in Bildern: Ägypten), Manniche, Sachs (History of Musical Instruments), Wilkinson, Polin, Sachs (Rise of Music), Hickmann (Orientalische Musik)

**The Two Horns:** Polin, Hickmann (Musikgeschichte in Bildern: Ägypten), Sachs (Wellsprings)

**Examples of Horns:** Hickmann (Musikgeschichte in Bildern: Ägypten)

## Chapter 4: Percussion Instruments

**Membrano Drums:** Wilkinson, Hickmann (Musikgeschichte in Bildern: Ägypten), Engel, Polin Abusir Drum: Sachs (History of Musical Instruments)

**Tambourine:** Wilkinson, Hickmann (Musikgeschichte in Bildern: Ägypten), Touma

**Non-Membrano Sticks:** Hickmann (Musikgeschichte in Bildern: Ägypten), Sachs (History of Musical Instruments)

**Clappers**: Wilkinson, Hickmann (Musikgeschichte in Bildern: Ägypten), Polin

**Sistrums (Sistra):** Wilkinson, Hickmann (Musikgeschichte in Bildern: Ägypten)

**Cymbals and Castanets:** Polin, Hickmann (Musikgeschichte in Bildern: Ägypten), Wilkinson, Sachs (History of Musical Instruments), Stanford/Forsyth

**Bells (Chimes):** Sachs (History of Musical Instruments), Polin, Engel Bells in museums and tombs: Hickmann (Musikgeschichte in Bildern: Ägypten)

**Xylophone:** Engel, Wilkinson

**Human Parts:** Wilkinson, Hickmann (Musikgeschichte in Bildern: Ägypten), Touma

## Chapter 5: Musical Performance

**Harmonic Hand**: Gadalla (Egyptian Rhythm, Egyptian Harmony), Vantoura, Sachs (Rise of Music), Hickmann (Orientalische Musik), Hickmann (Musikgeschichte in Bildern: Ägypten)

**Written Sounds**: Plato, Engel, Fétis, Stanford/Forsyth, Burney

**Rhythmic Timing:** Plato, Moore, Burney, Levy &

LeVarie, Sachs (Rise of Music), Gadalla (Egyptian Rhythm), Polin

**Moods and Modes:** Moore, Plato, Gadalla (Egyptian Rhythm)

www.ingramcontent.com/pod-product-compliance
Lightning Source LLC
Chambersburg PA
CBHW071518040426
42444CB00008B/1701